Breakthrough Mentoring in the 21st Century:

A Compilation of Life Altering Experiences

by Walter R. McCollum, PhD

Published by

McCollum Enterprises, LLC

Dr. Walter R. McCollum

Fort Washington, Maryland

ISBN 978-0-9791406-4-8

Dedication

"And we know that all things work together for good to them that love God, to them who are called according to his purpose." —Romans 8:28

Thank you God for being my ultimate mentor. Because of your mentorship, I am walking in my purpose and passion. Thanks for allowing me the opportunity to be a mentor to so many around the world. I will continue to let my light shine so that others can see your good work through me and give to you the praise and honor that you so richly deserve.

To my grandfather, Walter D. McCollum, Sr., in loving memory. Thanks for being my mentor, role model, and brother in Christ and for providing me with the foundation that helped me grow into the man I am today.

To my mentors who saw potential in me. Thanks for your guidance, leadership, encouragement, and love. I am so grateful. Your example has helped me mentor others academically, professionally, and culturally.

This book is dedicated to all mentors who are impacting social change in the lives of others. Continue passing the mantle.

"I can do all things through Christ which strengthens me."—Philippians 4:13

Invictus

William Ernest Henley (1849? 1903)

Louis Untermeyer, ed. (1855? 1977) Modern British
Poetry, 1920

OUT of the night that covers me,
Black as the Pit from pole to pole,
I thank whatever gods may be
For my unconquerable soul.

In the fell clutch of circumstance
I have not winced nor cried aloud
Under the bludgeonings of chance
My head is bloody, but unbowed.

Beyond this place of wrath and tears
Looms but the Horror of the shade
And yet the menace of the years
Finds, and shall find, me unafraid.

It matters not how strait the gate,
How charged with punishments the scroll,
I am the master of my fate:
I am the captain of my soul.

Acknowledgments

To my mother, Katherine B. Garner, and my father, Walter D. McCollum, Jr. Thanks for loving me unconditionally.

To my family members, colleagues, and friends. Thanks so much for the continued love and support you provide to help me stay focused while traveling through my journey. I am most grateful.

To Dr. Marilyn Simon and all the mentors who have had some part in shaping my life. I am indebted to you forever.

To my students at Walden University. Thanks for such a profound experience and opportunity to mentor you. I have learned just as much from you as you have from me. Keep pursuing your educational endeavors and passing the torch to those coming behind you.

To the Salem Zion Baptist Church Family. Thanks for keeping my grandfather's spirit and legacy alive.

Special thanks to my editor, Toni Williams. Thank you so much for supporting this book project. You are a gem! I am very grateful.

Father God, in the name of Jesus, thank you for my life, health, and strength. Thank you for grace and mercy. Thank you for healing power. Thank you for your reverence. Thank you for your omnipotence. Thank you for peace, love, and joy. Thank you for your protection. Thank you for my family and friends and the support they continue to provide me. Thank you for the favor you continue to place on my life. I am so grateful. Thank you for your darling son Jesus, who died on the cross so that we may have abundant life. Thank you for Calvary. Thank you for the bright and morning star. You are worthy and have all power in your hands to do all righteous things. For you are God and God alone. There is none above you, beneath you, nor beside you. How Excellent is your name in all the Earth. Thank you for yet another opportunity to put pen to paper. I pray that it will be received as a tool of inspiration to both mentors and mentees alike. Thank you for allowing me to accomplish my educational endeavors. Thank you for my spiritual gifts and my light that shines so that others can see your good works. Thank you for defining and confirming my purpose in life and supplying me with the tools to employ it. All of these blessings I pray in Jesus' name. Amen.

Table of Contents

Preface

The purpose of this book is to serve, at an initial glance, two functions. Primarily, using research and experience, I will show how adopting a formal mentoring process and formula can impact change and produce positive results in the lives of others. The formula is *breakthrough mentoring = emotional intelligence × structured process × measures > the amount of time spent with the mentee* (BM = EQ × SP × M > the amount of time spent with the mentee). Second, but with as much importance, I will also provide a compilation of life altering experiences from mentors and mentees alike, as they share their stories of how adopting and embracing a structured mentoring process produced positive outcomes in their lives.

In Greek mythology, Mentor was the son of Alcumus and, in his old age, a friend of Ulysses. When Ulysses left for the Trojan War, he placed Mentor in charge of both his son, Telemachus, and his palace. In modern usage, *mentor* has come to reflect this persona of a trusted friend, counselor, or teacher – usually a more experienced person. A mentee is a person who receives guidance and support from a successful, more experienced person in order to reach his or her personal and professional goals.

Growing up in the South as an only child in a single-parent household, I learned the importance of having a mentor. My paternal grandfather was my mentor and provided me with the mentorship I needed as a young boy that would eventually become my passion and purpose in life and would charge me to instill values, morals, principles, and the spirit of servanthood in others coming behind me. I am convinced that awareness of servanthood in my childhood years heightened my developing high emotional intelligence (EQ) in my adult years.

According to Cooper (2007), EQ is the cousin of intellectual intelligence (IQ); it is the ability to sense, understand, and effectively apply the power and acumen of emotions as a source of human energy, information, connection, and influence. EQ already exists in all of us because we are creatures comprised of emotions, because every experience results in some emotional response. What remains a significant opportunity for learning is the ability to recognize, label, and process emotions – our own and those of others – to achieve desired outcomes. EQ is a critical skill for the successful management of the diverse (across several dimensions) workforce that is evolving in the 21st century. EQ is a critical component in the process of breakthrough mentoring and something that is crucial to the personal and professional development of mentees. As you review the components of EQ below, consider how they apply to your mentoring journey as they are required ingredients for breakthrough mentoring in the 21st century.

Self-Awareness	The ability to recognize and understand your moods, emotions, and drives, as well as their effects on others.
Self-Regulation	The ability to control or redirect disruptive impulses and moods. The propensity to suspend judgment to think before acting.
Motivation	A passion to work for intrinsic reasons that go beyond money or status. A propensity to pursue goals with energy and persistence.
Empathy	The ability to understand and relate to the emotional makeup of other people. Skill in treating people according to their emotional reactions.
Social Skill	Proficiency in managing interpersonal relationships and building interpersonal networks. An ability to find common ground and build rapport with others.

The mentoring process, a structured process (SP), by its very nature is a journey and although there is a beginning and an end, the portion between the two is where the real growth occurs. The intent of the structured process is to make the journey less treacherous for both the mentor and the mentee. Mentoring is a long-term, one-on-one relationship based on mutual trust that is focused on the mentee's professional and personal development. Mentoring includes techniques from other developmental activities such as training and coaching but provides a depth and breadth those other methods cannot.

As you read this book, you will be inspired by stories of mentors and mentees. I urge you to reflect on what is happening in your current mentoring relationships, whether you are a mentor or a mentee. Then, evaluate the the components of the breakthrough mentoring formula (emotional intelligence, structured process, and measures) and determine if they are embedded in your mentoring. If you find there are gaps in your mentoring based upon your analysis, make the necessary adjustments to render the experience more meaningful and results oriented.

Introduction

"Give a man a fish and you feed him for a day. Teach a man to fish and you feed him for a lifetime."
--Chinese Proverb

There are nine phases in the breakthrough mentoring structured process (SP). The phases build upon each other to create an entire journey representing the span of the mentor–mentee relationship. However, everyone is different, and each mentee might prefer to take a different route. A description of each phase is noted below.

(1) Establishing a Path

Establishing a Path prepares the mentor and mentee for the mentoring relationship. This orientation phase helps both the mentor and the mentee learn about each other, so a strong relationship can be established. The more prepared the mentor and mentee are, the more beneficial the mentee's experience will be.

(2) Beginning the Journey

Beginning the Journey ensures the mentor is in the right frame of mind to facilitate the mentoring process. It is important that mentors continuously stay in facilitating mode and not direct, preach, or lecture mentees. The mentor should begin by establishing a climate for learning and establishing an effective relationship with the mentee. This phase is intended to provide an overview of how to begin the mentoring journey successfully.

(3) Planning the Route

In this phase, the mentor will assess the specific needs of the mentee using various assessments, questions, tools, and techniques. The mentor should listen carefully to the words of the mentee and read between the lines to fully understand the needs. This phase explains how to assess needs and listen with empathy.

(4) Traveling Together

This phase deals with establishing trust and building rapport so that the mentor and mentee work together toward the mentee's goals.

(5) Moving in the Right Direction

During this phase, the mentor and mentee agree on goals and ways to work together to reach those goals. The mentee is reminded to revisit the goals throughout the mentoring journey, so that a consistent effort is made toward reaching them.

(6) Preventing Roadblocks

This phase explains what to do when roadblocks or obstacles occur and resistance appears. The phase provides ideas for preventing and overcoming these and other challenges and continuing to move forward.

(7) Becoming a Guide

At this phase in the journey, the mentor takes on the role of a guide and facilitates ongoing developmental progress toward the established goals. The mentor's primary role in this phase is to provide thoughtful feedback and assistance to the mentee.

(8) Becoming a Confidante

By this phase in the journey, the mentor will have become more of a friend than he or she might have initially expected. The mentee will rely on the mentor for guidance in the professional and personal realm.

(9) Becoming a Lifelong Learner

Becoming a Lifelong Learner brings closure to the mentoring relationship. During this phase, both parties reflect on the experience and determine areas that might need further development. The last phase in the journey reinforces the commitment to a habit of lifelong learning. There are logical times when each of these phases will occur. Naturally, some mentees might need a longer or shorter period of time devoted to each, depending on the issue being addressed, the needs of the mentee, and so forth. Adjust the length of these phases as necessary to meet the needs of mentees, but be sure *not* to skip over any of the phases in the journey.

In *Establishing a Path*, the onset of the mentoring relationship is the best time to establish expectations with the mentee. To clarify these expectations, ask questions such as the following:

(1) Why are you interested in being mentored? How will you benefit from being mentored?

(2) What kind of progress would you like to make and in what areas? What would be a successful outcome in each area?

(3) What would be the most positive outcome for you personally? Professionally?

(4) What concerns, reservations, or fears do you have?

Mentors can help mentees by articulating expectations up front. At the beginning of the relationship, let the mentee know that you will not know all the answers, but you will act as a sounding board for trying out ideas beforehand, without risk, and you will provide support and encouragement in helping the mentee identify and solve his or her own problems.

In *Beginning the Journey*, the quality of the mentoring relationship depends on the extent to which the mentor and mentee come to know, respect, and trust each other. Mentees gain a stronger sense of self-worth when they realize the extent to which a mentor is willing to invest time and energy with them. To establish a climate for learning, the mentor should start by learning as much as possible about the mentee (without asking about specific personal details, of course). The time spent at the beginning is well worth the effort once the journey begins. Also be certain to listen and accept without judgment everything the mentee has to say. By doing so, the mentor will earn the mentee's trust over time. To ensure that a positive mentoring relationship is developed at the onset, the mentor can establish a climate for learning by doing the following:

(1) Remind yourself that adults learn by connecting their present experiences to past experiences.

(2) Adults learn best through experience, not through lectures.

(3) Adults like to have control of their own decisions and their own lives; they do not like being told what to do.

(4) Adults need to be able to immediately apply what they are learning.

(5) Adults respond to learning when they are motivated to do so.

In *Planning the Route*, take some time to delve into the mentee's specific needs by asking questions such as the following:

(1) What are your strengths?

(2) What are your developmental needs?

(3) What are your personal aspirations?

(4) What are your career aspirations?

(5) What specific challenges do you face consistently?

(6) What concerns do you have about the future?

(7) What do you want to accomplish as part of the
mentoring process?

First, ask the mentee to think about his or her
strengths. "What are two or three strengths on which you
would like to build and develop further, or for which you
would like to receive more recognition, or be able to use
more effectively in your current or future roles?" Next, ask
the mentee to identify two or three developmental needs on
which he or she would like to work. This might be based
on an area the mentee views as a potential liability or
weakness or it might be the result of feedback he or she has
received, changes the mentee sees in the workplace; or an
area in which the mentee is interested in growing to meet
the requirements of future roles.

Be certain the mentee understands that the needs
defined in the beginning are an important step in the
process and will be the focus during the journey. The
mentor might also want to revisit the mentee's needs after
significant progress has been made. This will ensure
continuous growth.

Ask the mentee to address career aspirations and
analyze his or her current and future interests. To set goals
with mentees, ask them first to think carefully through their
motivators. Ask them to determine what really motivates

or drives them. These factors are important to consider in relation to their career, as what drives them in their personal life must be aligned with their career motivators to avoid internal conflicts. Ask mentees to explore their career interests and motivations, as well as their most recent performance feedback and other available feedback to see if they are consistent.

Listen to what a mentee is saying by reading his or her words, but also connecting those words to what he or she said previously. Practice active listening throughout the mentoring process. Follow these guidelines to ensure active listening:

(1) Ask open-ended questions.

(2) Paraphrase.

(3) Use reflective communication, such as, "Remember when we discussed . . ." and relate what you are saying back to a previous communication.

(4) Use encouraging statements.

Empathic listening goes a step further than active listening. Empathic listeners try to hear emotions as well as words. Tune into a person's feelings as well as his or her words by doing a *feeling check.* That is, you can make a statement that interprets how you think the person might be feeling.

A professional attitude goes a long way in cementing a good relationship with the mentee. Mentors can do their part to convey an attitude of respect and acceptance by following these recommendations:

(1) Maintain an objective outlook.

(2) Consider the mentee's points of view.

(3) Express your confidence in the mentee.

(4) Encourage the mentee to express his or her ideas.

In *Traveling Together,* people will only follow those whom they believe are credible and worthy of their trust. Trust is the key in bonding a mentor and a mentee together. Trust is based on actions rather than words. You can say that you trust people, but if your actions do not back up those words, distrust is created. Giving mentees the sense that you respect them communicates or conveys a message of trust. Mentors should treat mentees as individuals, acknowledging them both personally and professionally.

Nothing can undermine trust faster than an individual who is incompetent, unethical, or uncaring.

Mentors need to respond in ways that clearly demonstrate their commitment in each of the areas that comprise trust. The components of trust are win/win, openness, honesty, and consistency.

Win/win is an important component of building trust. If people feel as though they are working together with you, rather than having to do what you say, then they will be much more cooperative. Let mentees know everything you know about the topic at hand, and let them know important and relevant things about you that make you who you are as a mentor. Remember that mentorship is personal. It is a personal relationship between the mentor and the mentee. How can they trust you if they do not know you as a person? Tell the truth. It is much easier to be consistent if you do not have to keep changing your story. Avoid mixed messages. Mentors who deliver a consistent message, based both on their words and on their actions, are trusted the most. Remember that no message *is* a message, albeit negative. If you say you will get back to someone on an issue or need to follow up on something, it is important that you see it through.

In *Moving in the Right Direction*, as a mentor, you must provide guidance throughout the journey. The important thing to remember is that this guidance can be obtained from many different sources – books, articles, exercises, advice, or simply questioning the mentee. Because you are facilitating the journey, you do not have to be the source of all knowledge. Instead, you must point the mentee in the right direction for finding the knowledge, skills, or behavioral change he or she seeks.

Create natural stopping points along the journey, which are simply places to rest and take stock of what your mentee has learned and what else the mentee might need to examine more closely. The stopping points or guideposts will probably become natural to you along the way. If they do not occur naturally, you simply could remind yourself to check in with your mentee as you finish each phase in the journey. At these points, take a breather. Take time for both you and your mentee to reflect on what has been learned. Ask questions such as the following:

(1) What has been the most important learning for you so far and why?

(2) What has been the least helpful and why?

(3) What would you like me to do differently?

(4) What else would you like to explore?

(5) What would you like to do better?

(6) What would you like to see more of?

(7) How can I help you with the next phase in your growth and development?

In the *Preventing Roadblocks* phase, the mentor and mentee might experience roadblocks. Roadblocks are obstacles that could hinder a developing relationship. There are obstacles unique to a mentor and obstacles that only a mentee will encounter. Below are a couple of examples of obstacles that could confront a mentor.

(1) A mentoring style that does not fit the mentee's needs: What happens when a highly organized mentor has a mentee with a relaxed work style? Or perhaps a creative mentee has a mentor who practices the "old school of thought"? What if an assertive mentor has a mentee with a reserved personality? Frustration can occur!

Your style of mentoring might not always match the needs of your mentee. Differences in styles between you and your mentee can pose an obstacle. Both of you need to understand each other's styles. Be flexible, but remember that disorganization and sloppiness impede improvement rather than foster acceptance. Setting clear expectations early is essential to avoiding many subsequent roadblocks and obstacles and the subsequent frustration.

Frustration might also occur when you do not adapt your style to meet the developing needs of your mentee. As your relationship evolves, your mentee's confidence grows, skills develop, and successes occur. You will need to adjust your mentoring techniques to keep in sync with your mentee's transformation. Your mentee might consider detailed directions or certain problem-solving strategies. Consider giving less and accepting more from your mentee as time goes on. After you evaluate your mentee and discover the required amount of guidance, you can determine what style is appropriate for your mentee.

(2) Insufficient time:

Another potential obstacle for mentors is insufficient time. Some mentors cannot seem to devote enough time to their mentee. Other commitments in your schedule might prevent you from spending time with your mentee. If you start to sacrifice time with your mentee because of other commitments, he or she might lose faith in you, and your mentoring relationship will suffer. Another obstacle involving time occurs when a mentor expects too much progress from the mentee in an unrealistic amount of time. Give your mentee time to grow professionally and to make mistakes along the way. Try not to be impatient with your mentee or expect too much too soon.

In *Becoming a Guide*, at times, there will be disagreements or a misunderstanding. Keep in mind that mentoring relationships are partnerships. It is important to accept the fact that you have a right to express yourself when you want to make adjustments to the mentoring relationship. However, it is just as important to make sure you resolve differences appropriately, professionally, and respectfully. Some examples of differences that might appear in a mentoring relationship include the following:

(1) Giving advice or guidance with which your mentee does not agree: Instead of arguing with your mentee, approach the situation with a sense of curiosity. Ask your mentee questions. For example, "That idea doesn't feel right, but I'm not sure why," or "It appears you do not agree with my advice and I would like to understand why."

(2) Your mentee misses an appointment you had scheduled: This is another time for curiosity. Instead of saying "You missed our meeting yesterday," approach your mentee with the goal of finding out information rather than

blaming. "I had on my calendar that we were scheduled to talk yesterday, did I get confused?"

(3) It feels as though your mentee wants you to tell them what to do, rather than relying on you as a sounding board and then solving his or her own problems. Often, mentees feel that you are supposed to give advice, make decisions, or solve problems for them. If this happens, remind the mentee of your role and clearly articulate what you can and cannot do.

One of the ways to successfully manage conflict is to provide regular constructive feedback, when it is needed. This technique might feel uncomfortable at first, but as time goes on, you will see it is an effective way to clear the air so that conflicts do not arise as frequently as before.

In *Becoming a Confidante*, every mentor must make a decision about how far the relationship extends and whether to get into personal decisions. That decision must be made by simply gauging your own comfort level with the subject matter.

Interpersonal problems are another matter altogether. Mentors should certainly help mentees improve in the area of interpersonal skills because social skills are an important part of emotional intelligence. To be an effective employee in any company, one must be sensitive and responsive to others and possess good interpersonal communication skills. These skills are just as important as technical competence. Yet, in most companies, technical expertise is what gets people hired. As a result, interpersonal skills are not focused on in the workplace to the extent they should be.

Studies show that if you remain too deeply rooted in your technical discipline, the likelihood of your communicating well with your customers and colleagues is not as strong. When appropriate, you might wish to review the following tips for developing the mentee's effective interpersonal skills:

(1) Never interrupt.

(2) Always acknowledge another person's ideas or suggestions.

(3) Be on time and keep meetings and appointments. This communicates your level of commitment.

(4) Use proper language and grammar. This increases your credibility.

(5) Try to add a social element to each interaction. This shows that you recognize the individual as a human being and not just as a mentee.

(6) Always acknowledge another person's ideas, regardless of whether you agree with them.

(7) Never blame others.

(8) Answer questions in a timely manner.

(9) It is okay to tell people that you are not sure of an answer. It is more professional to check and get back to them with the correct information rather than make something up.

(10) Always try to determine the feelings and attitudes that accompany information sharing.

In *Becoming a Lifelong Learner*, by understanding the root causes of an issue you will be in a strong position to implement a series of effective changes to resolve the problem. Root cause analysis requires an analyst to investigate why a certain outcome or result has been achieved. Usually these techniques are applied to failures or process breakdowns. It also is useful to understand why something was a success so that any lessons can be learned and replicated in the future. Here are some questions to ask the mentee:

(1) Have you identified the cause of the symptoms?

(2) Have you identified the problem behind the problem, or underlying cause (i.e., why the problem initially occurred)?

(3) Have you prioritized the factors that caused the problem to occur in terms of their contribution?

Measurements (M) are required ingredients to determine the success of the mentoring process. When the time comes that the mentor feels he or she no longer contributes to the needs of the mentee, when the mentee has achieved his or her goals, or when the mentee no longer has a need for mentoring, it is time to end the relationship. Ending the mentoring relationship well is important to the mentor's continued success, as first impressions and last impressions are what we remember most about others. Make your last impression a positive one.

Here are some tips to end your mentoring relationship on a positive note and measure its success:

(1) Be clear about why you and/or the mentee want to end the relationship. If the mentee has achieved his or her goals, celebrate! Let your mentee explain how you have helped him or her and show his or her appreciation.

(2) If the mentee is ending the relationship for other reasons, ask for an explanation. Perhaps the relationship is not moving the mentee forward and he or she would like to spend time engaging in other professional development activities.

(3) If you are ending the relationship for other reasons, let your mentee know the reason. Perhaps the relationship is no longer satisfying to you as a mentor, and you would like to utilize your time more productively.

(4) Regardless of the reason for ending the relationship, it is important to acknowledge what you and the mentee have accomplished,

provide the mentee with clear and constructive feedback about what he or she did well and what the mentee might continue to work on for continued growth and development. Remember a mentoring relationship is not like a marriage or other long-term commitment; the goal is to help the mentee move forward in his or her career and life goals.

(5) Revisit your purpose.

(6) Revisit the original goals established by you and your mentee.

(7) Revisit the mentoring agreement.

(8) This is a time for learning from both the good and the not-so-good experiences. Remember to learn from both.

Breakthrough mentoring in the 21st century requires a calculated process, such as *BM = EQ × SP × M > the amount of time spent with the mentee*. Although Kram (1985) observed early on that individuals actually have a constellation of developmental relationships, it was not until social network theory was brought to the study of mentoring that there emerged a language and method for describing and understanding the multiple sources of support. The social network perspective provides an important framework for understanding the dimensions of developmental networks, such as the range of sources from which individuals receive developmental help and the emotional closeness and frequency of communication in these relationships.

The mentoring stories in this book are inclusive of the highlighted ingredients in breakthrough mentoring. As a result of embracing and adopting $BM = EQ \times SP \times M > $ *the amount of time spent with the mentee,* the outcome is more likely to be positive. Also, the amount of time spent with the mentee is likely to decrease when a structured process embedded with emotional intelligence and measures are applied to a mentoring relationship. This is due, in part, to the great emphasis of emotional intelligence applied to the process and the continual communication and feedback provided to the mentee throughout the process.

References

Cooper, J. B. (2007, June). *Emotionally intelligent supervision: An examination of the role of* emotional intelligence *on the development of the supervisory working alliance.* Program presented at the Third International Interdisciplinary Conference on Clinical Supervision, Buffalo, NY.

Kram, K. E., & Isabella, L. A. (1985). Mentoring alternatives: The role of peer relationships in career development. *The Academy of Management Journal, 28,* 110-132.

1
Toye Latimore, Public Servant

"You must be the change you want to see in the world."
—Mahatma Gandhi

The 21st century is known for technological advancements that have afforded us opportunities and challenges. Through it all, we continue to visualize who we are, why we are here, and where we are going. To move forward in life's journey, it is incumbent upon each person to take responsibility for his or her past, present, and future. As a public servant for 30 years, I took advantage of the technological advancements that helped me to examine my path, goals, and aspirations. Public trust positions provide the foundation for individuals to persevere if the individuals take control of their career and map out the road to success. However, having a public trust position requires that each individual embody the confidence, assistance, and constructive criticism of someone who has his or her best interest at heart. For me, that someone was Mr. Keith Webster, a senior executive service member with the Department of Defense. As a senior leader, I had to regain my footing and select an individual who I wanted to emulate as well as guide me through the ranks.

This was not an easy task, as we all strive to achieve greatness. We all want to be like Colin Powell, Oprah Winfrey, or Nelson Mandela. These are all inspiring leaders who have achieved greatness. Thus, as a person who has a high regard for and a thirst for leadership, I had to reach for someone who was serious minded, was structured, envisioned all of the qualities above, and was within my purview. In addition, I wanted someone who was interested in my goals and who would share their life experiences, vision, and aspirations. This is what mentoring is all about. It is the fundamental theory of connecting oneself with someone who has goals, who believes in a vision, and who helps that person to aspire to be a Colin Powell, Oprah Winfrey, or Nelson Mandela. Mentoring results in finding your inner self, self-gratification, charting your path to success, and defining your purpose in life. Mentoring also requires hard work, perseverance, determination, and resiliency.

Mentoring is making a true impact on your life, your mentee's life, and your mentee's personality and ensuring that the individual makes an impact that affects social change. In addition, the dynamics of mentoring must continue so that others can refine their skills and utilize them in a positive manner. Mr. Webster was that individual for me. As a senior executive service member, he always made the time to sit and talk, provided guidance and constructive criticism that would eventually help me gain a position with more responsibility, and was never judgmental. Even though he had a political position, he was an individual who never let politics define his character.

Mr. Webster emulates the leadership principles of many leaders. He has a vision, is emotionally connected, has a structured personality, thinks strategically, and empowers people, which allows a person to measure his or her progress, and does not hesitate to counsel or give advice when mistakes are made. He refines this method by taking the time with a concerted effort to continually evaluate the individual to ensure that he or she is raising the bar. He embodies all the qualities of a good mentor, leader, person and public servant. He has a low tolerance for what one cannot do as his theory is anyone can do anything if they put their mind to good use. Therefore, he makes a person feel positive even in a negative situation.

Making time to share experiences, shadowing those experiences, and teaching those experiences were some of the activities that Mr. Webster displayed while mentoring me. It was evident that he enjoyed this partnership because he displayed compassion and was always positive. Mentoring is a partnership in which people continually learn from one another and share knowledge to enhance the characteristics and capabilities of one another. As an employee, I learned so much from this man that I gave back what was given to me and became a mentor myself. As a result of my mentoring experience, I am an individual who has persevered through much adversity, envy, and political backlash. Through it all, I always remembered who I was, where I was going, and why I was here. Currently, I mentor six interns with the Department of the Army, and it has been such a rewarding experience.

In addition, I am developing a mentoring program for our agency so that others can enjoy winning the hearts and minds of present and future employees. I have been a mentor for 8 years for various employees who have come from diverse backgrounds. This experience has allowed me to sit with each individual, to understand their culture, and to determine who they were, where they were going, and why they are here. It requires attention to detail, quality time, getting to know the individual, and providing feedback to questions posed. As a result, the mentees are very grateful, have moved on to positions of greater responsibility, and two are currently working toward their PhDs. This mentoring process could not have come to fruition without mapping out key goals within a certain time frame. I am a big advocate of projecting career progression via a timeline and meeting with my mentees biweekly to chart and monitor their progression. If one does not take control of his or her career, then no one else will.

This refinement results in self-satisfaction and self-awareness as well as determining if specific goals are being met. The results are exemplified by the expressions on their faces when a major milestone is met. In return, I feel good as a person that I was able to help, shape, and lead someone toward the path of wholeness. As a mentor, I have found that I have to be passionate as well as considerate and have the belief that anyone can attain a goal with hard work and dedication to the cause. Anything less is unacceptable. Mentoring is about listening to challenges, struggles, stories, and significant emotional events and turning these events into positive reinforcements for the future. Mentoring involves having an understanding of people and of how touching the lives of many can lead to a simple connection. That connection is the key that opens the door to future possibilities.

Prior to Mr. Webster becoming my mentor, my mother was my mentor. As a result of my mother mentoring me, I also chose to give back in her honor. As a single mother of five children, she had the highest regard for integrity and values. She did not have a college education but had the mind-set of a college student who had graduated summa cum laude. She was very smart and taught herself math, English, and philosophy. She also had a passion for the musical arts. However, due to financial constraints and rearing five children, I felt she was deprived of these accomplishments because of the choices that she made. For that, I have vowed to achieve each and every academic degree in memory of my mother because as my mentor, she displayed confidence and strived for education when she could not acquire it. Nothing was ever too hard and she had a disdain for pity parties regarding why one could not make great strides in life.

As a parent, my mother inspired all of us to embrace education. She constantly sat with us and studied, quizzed my siblings, mandated that the Bible be our guiding philosophy in life, and insisted that we not judge others. She was a woman who stood at 4'11" and carried a big stick. One dared not cross her. She was stern, self-confident, and motivated, and nothing was ever too hard. My mother mentored me for 45 years until she went home to be with the Lord in July 2002. Even through adulthood, she continued to chart my path, providing critical advice and constructive criticism. If I were on the path of making a mistake, she would let me make the mistake unless it was detrimental to my heath. She felt that one can only learn from their mistakes and not from their successes.

I often wondered why she did this, especially if she had prior experience. However, she once advised that life is not a path of doing everything right, but a path of getting it wrong so one could get it right. For that, I am eternally grateful for her direction and guidance. After her death, I had to question my goals and aspirations because I felt that I had nothing to live for. Many times I had to ask myself, Who Am I? After much thought, I determined that I am an individual with the highest regard for integrity, honest, hardworking, tenacious, and mild mannered and I have zero tolerance for disrespect. These are some of the words that I would use to describe myself as a mentor to several mentees. As a child who was reared by a single parent and who had little to eat and drink, I have aspired to rise above poverty, appreciate opportunity, and thank my heavenly father for all that I have.

My family did not have much and my mother tried religiously to provide for five children every day. My sister and I attended college and my brothers all chose different paths; nevertheless, all are doing as well as can be expected. My sister is working on her second PhD, and I my first. I am an individual who cared deeply for my ailing mother while pursuing my master's degree, raising two sons, and keeping my marriage alive. During this time, I encountered depression while watching the one woman who provided for me and gave me hope slip away in despair. In addition, I was reaching the pinnacle of my career in the leadership arena, which became very challenging and demanding upon my time.

I was able to balance it all and came through the many storms that descended on my doorstep, including caring for an ailing father who was never there while I was growing up. Who am I? I am a mentor, an individual who strives for perfection, always helping others even when I cannot help myself, and I try my best to not be judgmental. Many times I fall short of this goal, but I reflect and refocus. I have only had one girlfriend in my entire life and we have been friends since kindergarten and we both are 50 years old today. I do not socialize, as I have never felt that I actually belonged to any group and I guess that is why I function so well with online classes. I interact, but face-to-face interaction is not mandatory. As a leader of 55 government employees, one might wonder how I acquired a leadership position with the above qualities. I approached this endeavor with the passion of guiding and mentoring, while keeping the window open for new opportunities. I have been married for 30 years and blessed with a great man who supports all of my dreams and possibilities.

I am here to challenge the unchallenged and chart my path to success. I am here to assist others in need and ensure that my children (currently ages 26 and 30) do what is right in life and never forget that at the end of the day, integrity is all that is left. I am here today because I had a great leader, mentor, and teacher in my mother who rests in peace but taught me the meaning of self-worth, hard work, determination, and dedication to family and a cause. We are here because we have a purpose, although those purposes may be different. I am here because this is where I want to be. I do not aspire to be anywhere else in life, but pursuing my PhD so I can name my price, so I can work for myself, so I can be a part of social change, and so I do not have to explain why I did not pursue a PhD.

To say that I will end up at a certain place is not guaranteed. I am clear about what I want out of life and can honestly say I want to teach at a college or university where I can mentor the young and old as well as make a difference. However, because of my 30 years in the federal sector thus far, I may return to the federal sector as an annuitant and teach at an acquisition university so that I can share my mentoring experiences and share how to be a good steward of the taxpayers' dollars. I am and will always be a mentor to help ensure that individuals receive direction and have a purpose. I know who I am, why I am here, and where I want to go. With those directions, I know I will achieve success because failure is not an option.

2
David Streat, Ret. Lt Colonel, USAF

"Where no wise guidance is, the people fall, but in the multitude of counselors there is safety."
—Proverbs11:14 Amplified Bible

As I look back over the last 30 years of my life, I realize that my passion for mentoring seemed to have come from a combination of things. One of my earliest recollections of being a mentor is talking to my brothers and sisters about different decisions they were making in their lives. Another side of my mentoring experience just comes from managing the day-to-day activities of life. Sometimes life can be so challenging that people can lose hope and never attain what God has planned for them. I had good mentors and, to some degree, I was in the right place at the right time. My redeeming quality might have been that mentoring was something that just seemed to happen. I also did not formally know what mentorship was all about until I entered the military in 1982.

My military experience played a major part in my development as a mentor. It also helped me to add to and further develop the foundation of my core beliefs. It gave me a solid vision of some characteristics a mentor should have. As far back as elementary and high school, I would always tell friends what I thought they should be doing, what classes they should be taking, and who to talk to if they were having problems in school or at home. Some folks would say that I was just being a big brother because I was the oldest child. But I like to think I had a natural inclination to motivate others to move in a direction they might not have thought about before. There is no doubt in my mind that my military experiences had a significant impact upon the development of my fondness for mentoring.

After basic training, I was given an assignment in Ramstein, Germany. A noncommissioned officer met me immediately upon my arrival at the airport in Frankfurt, Germany. I'll call him Charley. Charley introduced himself to me as my sponsor. This was my formal introduction to mentorship because Charley explained to me that any questions or problems I had adjusting to my new surroundings, the local culture, or the military in general he would be the point of contact to answer those questions. This was the beginning of my formal mentorship development because I was new to the military, in a foreign country, didn't speak the language, didn't know the monetary system, and I definitely didn't know the cultural traditions. I was very dependent on my sponsor, particularly the first 6 to 8 months in the country.

However, as my time in Germany increased and I got more comfortable, I felt more confident and leaned on my sponsor/mentor less. The longer I stayed in the military, the more my duties and responsibilities expanded. Being a mentor became more than just answering a few questions. It felt more like a family connection. As a mentor, you develop a family atmosphere and mentality, which is why breakthrough mentoring in the 21st century requires the understanding and acknowledgment that mentoring is not about you. It really is about those you are mentoring. I have been mentoring people for more than 25 years, but at the same time, many have mentored me. The most satisfying thing that led me to getting more involved in mentoring was the notion that I could be involved in something bigger than I could ever imagine.

The military pushes you to constantly be your best, be accountable, and put others first, but being involved with someone's life is not something one can take lightly. Those principles drive me to be the best person and mentor that I could possibly be. To be a leader in war, you must be able to mentor and motivate people. In basic training, the systematic process of breaking down and rebuilding my mental models allowed me to develop a foundation for future mentorship development. Another key to my mentorship development is that I acquired valuable life-lessons in areas such as self-development, leadership, accountability, commitment, loyalty, dedication, and respect for others. Leadership, accountability, dedication, and respect should be the foundation that other mentoring principles can be built upon.

Because military folks have many responsibilities given to them and are held accountable to high standards, it puts pressure on individuals to perform at their best at all times. The responsibilities also demand that they mature as a person and as a part of a larger team. I believe that it is in this setting that mentorship really stands out and sets the foundation for future development. There were lessons in basic training that affected my understanding of how leaders are supposed to conduct themselves. I had no idea of how much it impacted me until much later in my career. For example, everyone in my unit had individual cleaning assignments they were responsible to complete. If someone did not do his part, the whole unit suffered for it. Those episodes taught me the value of responsibility, accountability, commitment, and dedication. Those are the same characteristics a mentor should have. Especially if he or she is to have a positive effect on the mentee.

Another outcome of being a mentor is the ability to have a direct impact on the community. I firmly believe that a mentor is a leader who continually develops his or her leadership capabilities. A mentor develops those skills by being better prepared to mentor through education, training, self-reflection, and an acknowledgment that there is always room to improve. Mentoring can take place in many different ways. I know there are tons of books that talk about the role of the formal mentoring process. But in the 21st century, one must throw the books out the window to some extent. Today, young people are not interested in what past generations were doing or even how they did it. To be a good mentor one must meet mentees where they are.

For example, today a mentor might have to use Facebook, Twitter, LinkedIn, or some other social network entity to communicate, guide, and direct a young mentee. Those social networking platforms are a very effective and efficient way to stay connected in the millennial's, Gen. Y's, and Gen. X's wired world. My 24-year-old son is a prime example. It seems the only way that I can communicate with him is by texting, Facebook, MySpace, or e-mail. He is always mobile; everything is always on a 24/7 cycle and portable in his world. I have to admit he does talk to me on occasion. In some corners of the mentoring spectrum, there is the idea that men cannot mentor women and vice versa. I say that is false. I have mentored women on several occasions. Women in high leadership positions have mentored me as well. For example, I have a female colleague who I have mentored for the past 5 years. My mentorship started because she wanted to know about my school. She also wanted to know how I was able to work and go to school at the same time. I started talking to her about developing an education plan and accomplishing future goals.

That led to talking about the avenues inside and outside of the organization that she could use to make her dreams come true. Because of our constant interaction, she has completed her associate's degree and is well on her way to getting her bachelor's degree. She also has plans to pursue her master's degree. My point is that it all depends on your perspective as to whether you can mentor someone of the opposite sex or not. Of course, I kept the relationship on a professional level at all times. I made sure that I was a professional whether I was a mentor or a mentee. An important key to mentorship is that you don't have to be the person's immediate supervisor, friend, or relative to mentor someone. You just have to be open to the possibility and opportunity to be a mentor. In fact, several female noncommissioned and commissioned officers mentored me while in the military. I did not know then how important it was to me that they took the time to talk to me about continuing my education and life after the military. The time they took mentoring me helped complete my plan of what I wanted to accomplish after I retired from the military.

However, mentoring is more than just talking to someone. Mentoring is being there to encourage, motivate, advise, counsel, constructively criticize, and empathize when needed. Mentoring is especially important when a mentee has gone through a divorce, lost a loved one, or experienced some other tough situation. It is in those times that a true mentor will shine. It will be even more critical in the future for mentors to understand who they are in order to communicate effectively with those they mentor. The development of a mentor's emotional intelligence will play a significant role in the future of mentorship. Emotional intelligence skills are not only important to understanding people who work for you, but that same understanding will be needed to advise, motivate, and guide the next generation of leaders.

3
Chernoh Wurie, Police Officer

"Keeping a commitment or a promise is a major deposit into the emotional bank account; breaking one is a major withdrawal"
—Stephen Covey

"No Police Authority" was the three red-letter words that kept on spinning in my mind as I walked into the Crime Prevention Unit (CPU). These words were printed in bold on my identification card. It was my first day as a police intern with the CPU. As much as I hated those three words, in order to fulfill my long-held interest in becoming a police officer, I had to complete a summer internship with the police department and complete my bachelor's degree in criminal justice. That summer in CPU turned out to be one of the most memorable and meaningful periods in my life.

One afternoon, I was in my cubicle filing case files when I heard strident laughter coming from the other end of the hallway. The laughter became louder and louder, I slunk to the corner of my cubicle attempting to be unnoticeable. One of my greatest humiliations was having every detective and crime prevention officer who walked by my cubicle read the words "No Police Authority" on my ID card. As the laughter went away, this suddenly gave me a sense of relief from being embarrassed.

To my surprise, the loud individual popped up right inside my cubicle and started asking me several questions. Each question was followed by the same loud and annoying laughter. I was very uncomfortable and I wanted this torture to end, but it did not. His last and final question was what are the red-letter words on your ID card? At this point, I was furious. I maintained my composure and read them to him: "No Police Authority." He laughed and walked away. I could hear his annoying laughter fading as he made his way to the other side of the office.

This incident happened 7 years ago, although I remember the incident it as if it happened last week. I really did not like this individual; little did I know that he would be my mentor and the most influential person in my professional and personal life. This individual was retired First Sergeant Anthony E Spencer (Paps) with the Prince William County Police Department.

Every morning following our first meeting, Paps would come by my cubicle and ask, "Chernoh, when are these words on your ID going to change from No Police

Authority to Police Authority?" After being very displeased for the first 3 weeks, I somehow developed a tolerating demeanor toward him. I actually started looking forward to him coming by my cubicle every morning. We became very close when I rode with him in his unmarked police cruiser. It was my first time in a police cruiser.

He was assigned to Criminal Investigations Division as the deputy commander. Within that short period, I told him where I was from, a little bit about my family migrating to the United States due to civil war, and my career aspirations. Strangely, he became fond of me and took me under his wing. I learned a lot about him during our ride alongs. I discovered that we had a lot in common: we could both relate to the hardships in life and both grew up in families in which resources were not readily available.

Three distinctive characteristics, encouragement, confidence, and discipline, described retired First Sergeant Anthony E Spencer. The concept of encouragement played a major role in our relationship. As an immigrant from the war-torn country Sierra Leone, my experiences had negatively affected my confidence in pursuing my dream. My mentor repaired my shattered confidence.

Encouragement—He gave me the most encouragement that a mentor could give a mentee. His most famous saying was, "Son! You have not come this far to be a failure." I often reflect on this particular statement. He was right; I was not going to let a minor insecurity stand in my way of pursuing my dream.

Confidence—Prior to attending the police academy, I would enter his office and solemnly express my concern of not making it through the academy. I would normally base my concern on the fact that I would be attending the academy with over 60% of prior military recruits. I was afraid that I would never compare to their standard. My mentor provided me with the confidence that I needed to attend the police academy.

Discipline—On one particular occasion, I was going to a sexual assault call with my mentor. Although I was not familiar with using a map, my mentor handed me the map and asked me to look up a street and navigate us to the destination. I felt nervous and humiliated. How could I tell my mentor who had given me so much confidence and encouragement that I did not know how to read a simple street map? My pride kicked in, and I pretended as if I knew how to read the map, but he soon detected my deception and gave me a fierce tongue-lashing.

"You ought to know this petty stuff Chernoh, how can you be a cop without knowing how to manually navigate these streets using your map?" I felt as if I had deceived him and let him down; his expectations of me had been affected. Over the next couple of hours, I taught myself how to read a map. That day I learned that my mentor could be encouraging and had confidence in me, but he could also be very strict. Because of his reaction to my lack of knowledge of map reading, I took the initiative to teach myself.

The basic structure I had with my mentor was twofold: a parental role model and a supervisor. I enjoyed both roles tremendously; however, as an intern and a mentee, it was difficult to decipher which role to adapt to at a certain time. Conversely, my mentor could distinguish these roles easily. One minute he was acting as a father figure giving me advice and the next he was being a strict supervisor who wanted what was best for his employee. During the weekends, he would invite me to barbecues at his place and other outings. I enjoyed these times as well;

we became very close and shared vital details about each other's lives.

On one distinct occasion, I saw an attractive woman and I asked my mentor, "Paps, what's up with her?" Unbeknownst to me, Paps told her that I wanted to talk to her. I was left alone with this beautiful woman in the kitchen to initiate a conversation and get to know her. I reverted to one of the many pieces of advice from my mentor: in such a situation, start with a compliment or with anything other than "I." I complimented her on her dress, her school achievements, and her sports achievements; we found common ground as we both played sports. Conversation quickly become easier. Thanks to Paps, I was able to initiate a conversation with an attractive stranger. Following this incident, Paps assumed numerous roles; by using a simple structure of mentoring me during personal life situations and professional life scenarios, his mentoring style was unique and very well presented.

Paps initially had a major goal for me, which was to successfully go through the police academy and become an excellent officer. His goals for me were based on my level of accomplishment. I had several goals, and after accomplishing them, he challenged me with more.

Although the goals seemed unrealistic at times, I am proud to say that they motivated me and thus far I have accomplished all his goals and expectations for me.

Paps wanted me to be the best; he wanted me to go beyond what he has done. He made that very clear to me. Even though Paps did not complete his college education, he encouraged me to further my postgraduate education. This was a unique experience because as an African who migrated from Sierra Leone, I am used to a culture that is predominantly about competition instead of collaboration. Just as Paps wanted me to go beyond his educational achievements, I have received similar encouragement from my biological father for about 25 years.

The life altering experience that resulted from this mentorship is that I was so deeply influenced by Paps that I have taken up the initiative of becoming a mentor myself. I am currently a mentor for the Big Brothers and Big Sisters Program. I am currently mentoring a young man who is 15 years old and in high school. He has the same issues that I had when I was his age. I can relate to him in numerous ways. I personally have the confidence that I will assist this young man personally, professionally, mentally, and spiritually.

4
Jodine Burchell, Senior Programmer/Analyst

"The future belongs to those who believe in the beauty of their dreams"

—Eleanor Roosevelt

I've always thought of myself as a self-sufficient person. I have worked since I was 16 and spent many of the past 28 years going to school to improve myself and my quality of life. Sure, I had emotional support from my family and friends, but I always knew I had to rely on myself and my own tenacity to achieve my goals. In 2007, 5 years after earning my master's in computer information systems, I reentered the world of academia. I enrolled at Walden University to get my PhD in management with an emphasis in information systems management. I had prepared myself for the journey assuming that I was on my own. I knew that at some point in my program I would be assigned a mentor who would become the chairperson for my dissertation. My understanding was that a mentor is much like an advisor or a guide through the process. I had no idea what the exact nature of that relationship might be, but I had faith that I would understand in time. I had faith that I would find a mentor who was perfect for me. I also assumed that I wouldn't need much from my mentor and I could finish the program mostly on my own.

As I started classes at Walden University, I kept my eyes and ears open, looking for someone I connected with who I could ask to be my mentor. I was immediately impressed by Dr. Walter McCollum, who was the professor for my first information systems management class. He was one of the few professors who gave me feedback even when I received an A on an assignment or paper. I had the distinct impression that he really cared about his students. A few months and a few classes later, I asked him to be my mentor and he agreed. At this point, my assumption was that a mentor is just an advisor, someone to chair my dissertation committee and guide me through the doctoral process. I soon came to understand that my assumption was very wrong.

I joined Dr. McCollum's forum a few months before I would actually start working on my Knowledge Area Modules (KAMs). KAMs are extensive research papers that some describe as mini dissertations or as scholarly writing practice in preparation for the dissertation. Dr. McCollum would be my assessor for the three KAMs that I had to complete before I could start working on my dissertation. Because I joined the forum while still taking classes and before I started my KAMs, I was free to participate and observe, but I had no real need for interaction with Dr. McCollum. In the forum, I saw students being supportive and engaged. I saw my mentor publically offering congratulations to students as they achieved their milestones. I saw him offer his time and direction any time it was needed and provide a promise to respond to e-mail within 48 hours. As I worked on my KAMs, I found that my mentor was very supportive, unselfishly offered his time, and returned assessments and comments as promised. I was amazed at Dr. McCollum's level of commitment to his students. It wasn't very long before I started to realize that I wasn't completely on my own on this journey.

At some point, Dr. McCollum started a peer mentor/mentee program for his forum. This program was designed so that students could actively support each other. I, as a newer student, could reach out to my peer mentor in an informal manner and ask questions about KAMs, the dissertation, or even the process of getting through my doctoral journey. This program was a perfect avenue for students to get support by talking to other students who were further along in the program. My mentor is always here for me if I need direction, but it was so helpful being able to connect with other students as well. I tested the waters. I asked the lead peer mentor, Shana, if I could call her and discuss some issues I was having. She happily agreed and we talked for at least 2 hours about KAMs and how she arrived at a dissertation topic.

I believe that it was that 2-hour conversation that left the biggest impact on me. It changed everything. I already knew that Dr. McCollum was exceptional as a mentor. I already felt lucky that he was my mentor. I already expanded my understanding of what a mentor actually is. In other words, I realized that Dr. McCollum was my actual mentor and not just an advisor or guide through the process. What I also realized was *my* contribution to the process. Until this point, I was looking at other people's roles as they pertained to me, but what about *my* role with respect to them? I realized that this is not a one-sided relationship. I was not the only one gaining from these interactions and relationships. I realized that I have something to give, something to contribute to others. I had to open up to accept what others had to offer into my life and realize what I could contribute to others as well. I realized that I am not alone in this process and I never was.

At some point, Dr. McCollum asked me if I wanted to be a peer mentor and I wholeheartedly agreed. By this time, I'd successfully finished one KAM and was working on my second. I received my assigned list of mentees and I reached out to each of them and offered to talk any time they needed support or had questions. Since then, I have had many wonderful conversations with my mentees. I can honestly say that the benefits from peer mentor/mentee relationships are not one-sided. I get such joy from the interactions that I have had with my mentees.

Dr. Shana Webster-Trotman finished her program and graduated a few months ago, and Dr. McCollum appointed me as the lead peer mentor. Since then, I've had the chance to reflect on what it really means to be a peer mentor. Until this point, I felt that all I did was open myself up to whatever gifts the universe had for me. I had no clear understanding of the characteristics of a good mentor. I had not formally considered the structure of the mentor–mentee relationship or how a successful mentorship is measured. When I considered the impact of mentoring in my life, I looked at two dimensions:

1. What impact has being a mentee had on my life?

2. What impact has being a peer mentor had on my life?

It was very hard to distinguish, because both have had a huge impact on my life. I would even venture to say that being a mentee and mentor jointly has impacted my life in a way that being either could not. There is a constant give and take and a mutual respect involved within the peer mentor–mentee relationship. Even when I am talking with fellow students, I realize that I am not an expert. I can offer my experience and what worked for me, but it's ultimately up to the students to find their way through the process and do what works for them, their area of interest, and the direction they need to take to be successful.

I realize that the characteristics of a faculty mentor will likely differ from those of a peer mentor. The measure of success would likely be different as well. Characteristics of a peer mentor–mentee relationship include a mutual respect, a give-and-take exchange where one might have more expertise in one area and can offer advice, assistance, and support, but either person or both can learn and benefit from the exchange. The qualities of the persons involved include a willingness to give of their time and to be open to making long-lasting friendships. While one person is obviously the peer mentor and one is the mentee, I believe the structure is both formal and informal. There are obvious assigned roles, but both are students and one just happens to be further along in the process than the other.

What are the measures of success in a peer mentor–mentee relationship? This question is complicated to answer. After all, there may be students who make it through the doctoral process without making peer connections. Obviously, students are required to interact with faculty mentors, but some students might check in with their peer mentor only because they are expected to. The success can be seen in the peer mentors and mentees who actively engage each other. Even if the peer mentor cannot answer the mentee's question, success is achieved if there is a positive interaction between the two. Obviously this is very simplistic. I cannot even say that every interaction with another student has been positive, but I can say without a doubt that the relationship with my faculty mentor, my past peer mentor, and my mentees has changed my whole perspective on life and learning. I no longer want to rely on my own tenacity to make it through. I like being able to rely on the support of others to keep me going. I like that others might be able to rely on me to get through tough times.

I no longer believe that my success is all my own. I owe a big part of it to those with whom I have formed these relationships and connections. I owe it to my faculty mentor, Dr. McCollum, who has led me through the doctoral process and taught me the joys of mentoring and being mentored. I owe it to my mentees who interacted with me and allowed me to be a part of their lives and their journey. I owe it to my mentees because they have allowed me to really see that maybe I can have an impact on others and their success. I am grateful to Dr. McCollum and everyone for helping me to realize that I am not alone in this process and I never was.

5
Cernata Catherine Stanton Morse, Management Consultant

"Human beings, by changing the inner attitudes of their minds, can change the outer aspects of their lives."
—William James (1842-1910)

I have had the distinct pleasure of experiencing the best of both worlds through mentor relationships. I have been the recipient of effective mentorship and I have been a mentor. Mentoring is a partnership between two persons or among many people. Both mentors and mentees must be committed to providing opportunities to learn from one another and leverage each other's experience on an ongoing basis to effectively develop personal, professional, and spiritual growth. Within the relationship, it will be clear that one person has more experience than the other; however, the uniqueness of mentoring is that all parties involved will enhance their experience in personal and professional growth, as well as spiritual intellect. The proverb "each one teach one" applies holistically in a mentorship relationship.

While living in a quiet community in Fairfax County, Virginia, I was blessed with the opportunity to impact social change. Within the community, as well as in most communities, there existed a distinct socioeconomic barrier between the classes of residents. The challenge was bringing the two communities together for the common good of the high school neighborhood. The community was comprised of students, faculty, parents, businesses, and faith-based organizations. The common goal within the community was to ensure the academic success of each student and provide the opportunity to achieve success while creating a sense of shared vision.

My relationship and passion for mentoring is embedded deep within my soul. There has always existed a burning desire to become an advocate for those less fortunate. I would be remiss if I did not acknowledge the development of such passion is solely attributed to my late mother, Mrs. Catherine V. Webb Stanton. Being raised in the 1960s in Alexandria, Virginia, I witnessed a culture of sharing, giving, and caring at an early age. I actually lived in a community where everyone knew everyone in their neighborhood and everyone helped one another. My immediate family was small, consisting of my father, mother, grandmother, sister, and nieces, but the religious foundation of a Christian faith was a daily part of our lives and we adhered to the love of God as our resource. Together we appreciated the simple things in life and never realized our socioeconomic level was poor. We always had food, clothing, and shelter, and even enough to share. My mother planted the passion of mentoring when I witnessed her willingness to share with those in the community who were less fortunate and her willingness to give. She would bake and share her baked goods with the homeless in the neighborhood. She was a seamstress and she'd use the remaining materials from her clients to make clothing for her family and the children in the neighborhood. And the one thing I remember most was her willingness to provide advice, encouragement, and a sense of hope to all those who were in her presence. She demonstrated the true role of mentoring in my presence and her beacon of light became my passion.

My mentoring experience entails over 20 years of student and community partnerships. Some of my earlier experiences started as a role model and mentor within my own children's public school community. I would mentor students one-on-one or within a group setting, in my home, as well as develop relationships with parents of at-risk students. One of the most rewarding mentoring successes was my ability to impact social change as the parent liaison representative of West Potomac High School in Fairfax County, Virginia. Under the leadership of the principal, Dr.

Henry R. Johnson, Jr. (West Potomac High School, 2001-2003), I was involved with several critical projects to increase the achievement of students and to involve parents in that process. I organized a mentoring program with the Fairfax County Police Department called Men of Honor, placing police officers in mentoring positions working with male African Americans and Hispanics. The objective was to develop relationships of academic and behavioral skills to impact social change. I organized various programs (rap sessions, tutoring, parenting development groups, and mentoring), as well as organized educational programs for the school community to ensure success. I witnessed students who never thought they could succeed waiting for my arrival at work to study with me. I witnessed the gleam of hope in their eyes as we completed college applications late at night in my office. I saw the tears of joy of parents who did not understand the administrative school culture. I felt the love, appreciation, and gratitude from the students and their families when the students graduated and enrolled in the armed services or received the acceptance letter from a college. This experience confirmed my purpose in life!

The success of my mentoring programs was measured by the success of the Class of 2004, the first graduating class at West Potomac held to the Virginia State

Board of Education Standards of Learning based on the No Child Left Behind Act of 2001. The Class of 2004 successfully graduated over 90% of the student body meeting the goals, which reflected a decrease in detention, suspension, and student dropout rates in 2004. Upon my departure from the Fairfax County Public School System, the success rate dropped to 76% the following year. Dr. Johnson stated, "I attribute the declines to [her] inability to devote the time and attention to the individual students and assist the parents because of accepting a new position in Montgomery County."

My passion for mentorship is driven by a motivation to inspire people to create the vision and possibility of achieving a purpose in life, even when the odds are stacked against them. My relationship with the students within the disenfranchised community not only provided the mentees with an opportunity to gain knowledge, experience and developmental skills in emotional and intellectual intelligence, but the relationships provided me the opportunity to enhance my communication and behavioral skills, appreciate diversity, develop relationships, and most importantly increase my accountability as a role model. The disenfranchised community impacted me personally. The interaction with the students, motivating, inspiring and giving them hope to reach for the impossible, helped me to analyze my possibilities in life. During this life-changing experience, I too was impacted by a few mentors. I was being motivated, encouraged, and inspired to overcome the obstacles of life and to identify the possibility of achieving a purpose in life. The students gave me hope and inspiration with each milestone of success and achievement. In 2004, under the mentorship of Dr. Johnson, I decided to forget about the past and reach for the future. Dr. Johnson encouraged me to consider fulfilling my academic goal by completing a bachelor of science degree in business management. I set out on my journey to complete the degree at the University of Phoenix, while working for Dr. Johnson.

As I pursued my journey of completing my degree at the University of Phoenix in 2004, one of my distinguished professors impacted my life, personally and professionally: Dr. Walter R. McCollum. Dr. McCollum was my professor at the University of Phoenix School of Business Management. From the first day of class, it immediately became apparent to me that Dr. McCollum was committed to the pursuit of academic excellence. Dr. McCollum demonstrated professionalism, authority, and integrity. I often used the phrase, "Dr. McCollum is firm, but fair." He portrayed a grand level of expectation and would often challenge his students to achieve academic excellence by reaching beyond their comfort zone. Dr. McCollum created a space of intellectual capability by creating possibilities.

Dr. McCollum developed our mentoring relationship by creating a space of trust, integrity, mutual respect and learning. Because of my previous experience mentoring at-risk youth, I understood the diverse dynamics of mentoring and foresaw that Dr. McCollum's expectations would be at a higher level of thinking. I had established a goal to earn my bachelor of science in business management, but Dr. McCollum created a vision of empowerment, opportunity, and possibilities beyond my then-current thinking. He challenged my vision of fulfilling academic excellence at the bachelor's degree level by motivating me to consider pursuing a PhD.

Dr. McCollum established a very clearly defined process of mentorship. He was my mentor and professor at the University of Phoenix and currently at Walden University. As my professor, he was able to measure my academic success, as I always maintained at least a 3.6

GPA. During our communication sessions, he would encourage me to think beyond my comfort zone and apply the knowledge, skills, and expertise I've gained throughout my academic and life journey. Dr. McCollum would create opportunities to demonstrate my growth and abilities in specific skill sets within the academic and professional environment. I participated in focus groups, performed as team lead, and worked in focus groups and cross-function teams. He also developed a peer-mentoring structure to ensure student success throughout both the master's and PhD programs. This type of model increases the student success rate by aligning peer mentors and mentees in a forum of accountability.

Dr. McCollum's standards of excellence are implemented throughout his mentoring relationship, as well as coursework. His philosophy and strategies of increasing intelligence capabilities are reflective of the quality of PhD students he has mentored. He defined the importance of the mentoring relationship, which was guided by mutual respect, spiritual passion, and integrity. He was accessible, but there was a respect for scheduling and timing. His professionalism was and still is the epitome of a world-class mentor. He expected all his mentees to consistently demonstrate respect, spiritual growth, academic excellence, and integrity throughout all aspects of life. He demonstrated the characteristics of a Christian, scholar, and mentor. I personally attribute his success as a mentor to his God-like characteristic to pour out his talents into God's people.

The mentoring relationship has granted both he and I an opportunity to enhance our level of expertise. Dr. McCollum humbly acknowledges his gratitude toward what he has gained through his mentoring relationships—some of which have been life-changing experiences. Through his mentoring leadership, he created a space of mutual respect, accountability, and integrity by empowering me as his mentee. Dr. McCollum has offered me sage advice, demonstrating the expectations and requirements of becoming a scholar and an ambassador of social change. As my mentor, advisor, and role model, he has invested time and energy in my development of becoming a PhD candidate.

Dr. McCollum identified the possibilities I could offer society in fulfilling my purpose in life. He ignited the hope with guidance, respect, optimism, and a vision. He provided a vehicle for change by demonstrating the positive outcomes of someone who has overcome life's obstacles and pursued academic excellence. He demonstrated his commitment by mentoring, tutoring, volunteering, and most recently participating in a mission trip to a foreign country to impact social change. Dr. McCollum has shared his knowledge, expertise, and experiences in life to inspire, motivate, and encourage me to continue to grow spiritually, personally, and professionally. He consistently creates opportunities to enhance learning and development by offering study and mentoring sessions, lectures, and exposure to experienced professionals. As his mentee, I have always embraced his in-depth knowledge, commitment, and dedication to social change. As a result of my mentoring relationship with Dr. McCollum, I have received my bachelor of science in business management from the University of Phoenix (3.7 GPA), I have received my master's in business administration in organizational leadership from Walden University (3.9 GPA), and I am currently enrolled in the PhD program in applied management and decision sciences: leadership and organizational change at Walden University (4.0 GPA), where Dr. McCollum is my faculty mentor and professor for 7100 Research Forum.

Mentorship requires dedication, commitment, and integrity to develop the relationships required to be a success in the mentoring process. Effective mentoring partnerships develop a mutual respect; embrace diversity; and inspire, empower, and motivate one another to identify visions of hope, reality, and possibilities. Within the relationship, everyone can inspire others to create the vision of fulfilling their individual life purpose. The relationship will challenge the individuals' emotional maturity, emotional intelligence, and emotional spirituality to encourage the affirmation of life. Dr. McCollum's vision of mentoring has impacted social change within my professional and personal environment. His inspiration, commitment, motivation, and leadership have created a vision and possibilities in fulfilling my life's purpose. Dr. McCollum's mentoring guidelines are rich with learning, support, reality, and shared experiences.

6
Vince Truett,
Management/Strategic Consulting

"It is not the critic who counts; not the man who points out how the strong man stumbles, or where the doer of deeds could have done them better. The credit belongs to the man who is actually in the arena."
—Theodore Roosevelt

In the fall of 1981, I entered Price High School (Atlanta, Georgia) as a ninth grader. The school had two guidance counselors—one for 8th, 9th, and 10th graders and one for juniors and seniors. Dr. Eula Cohen was the guidance counselor for juniors and seniors. It would be 2 years before we would communicate on a regular basis, but little did I know at the time that she would become one of the most important individuals in my life.

As Dr. Cohen would learn 2 years later, my circumstances were unique. Like most Price High students, I came from a poor background—either living in a housing project or in close proximity to one. However, my parents were able to send me to two Catholic elementary schools for fourth through eighth grades. Given that private high schools were considerably more expensive than private elementary schools, my parents could not afford to send me to private school beyond the eighth grade. Thus, I attended the high school closest to our home—Price High. This was not an easy decision for the Truett family.

Shortly after beginning my junior year, I had my obligatory first meeting with Dr. Cohen. We began our conversation by discussing the fact that her husband and my father had known each other for many years—going back to the 1950s. We then drifted into conversations about my academic record and whether I wanted to attend college. I was an honor student who had plans to continue my education beyond high school. Dr. Cohen emphasized the importance of taking the Preliminary Scholastic Aptitude Test (PSAT) and scouting for scholarship money during my junior year. Like most of my peers, I nodded and looked at the clock to see how much time was remaining for our session.

I did not take my PSAT discussions with Dr. Cohen very seriously. As we had additional meetings, she planted seeds such as taking a PSAT prep course or purchasing a preparation guide so that I could prepare during the months leading up to the exam. I did neither and paid a huge price. I still vividly recall the day that I received my PSAT score in the mail. I also remember how dejected I felt after seeing my score. My score was an embarrassment to myself, my family and all my current and former teachers. How do I fix this? What do I need to do to ensure these results are not repeated next year with the SAT? How do I approach Dr. Cohen? These were just some of the questions that I asked myself in the hours after receiving my PSAT score. While I did not know all the answers, one thing was clear: I had to schedule a meeting with Dr. Cohen as soon as possible!

My next meeting with Dr. Cohen was quite different than the previous meetings. This meeting was much more focused. We discussed strategies and options. While she thought that I should take the PSAT again during my junior year, I could not face another potential failure during the same school year. However, I vowed that I would soon begin preparing for next year's SAT. I also promised to spend the summer preparing for the SAT.

As a high school junior, I had thoughts on my mind other than academics. During my junior year, I had a conversation with the teacher who advised the school's Student Government Association (SGA). He asked me whether I was interested in running for SGA president. I told him that I was not interested in the least. As one of my former teachers, the SGA advisor knew me quite well. In some respects, I was a television and he had the remote control. Within seconds of stating that I was not interested, he said, "You have to be tough to be an SGA president. If you don't have the stomach for the position, I agree that you should not run." What? Is he suggesting that I am a coward? Me? Vince Truett? I will show him! All these thoughts were racing through my mind. However, I knew that it would be inappropriate to offer a knee-jerk response that I would pursue the SGA presidency. Before I made a final decision, I had to speak to Dr. Cohen.

Within short order, I was meeting with Dr. Cohen to discuss whether I should run for SGA president. I now realize that our relationship was evolving. Our discussions were no longer limited to academics. I now viewed her as a mentor who could guide me in the right direction. During the meeting, I was quite candid about not having the desire to run for SGA president. Dr. Cohen noted that there were other considerations. For example, could I develop a platform and assemble a team that would be committed to representing the best interests of Price High students? Absolutely! After responding to a series of questions, Dr. Cohen said, "I think you would make a great SGA president." Within 24 hours, I informed the SGA advisor that I would run and that I would spend the next few days assembling a team. I can still see Dr. Cohen's beaming smile on the day that the results were announced. She was very proud that I would be the next SGA president at Price High School.

Although Dr. Cohen and I talked a lot during my junior year, we talked considerably more during my senior year. As I promised during the previous school year, I did prepare for the SAT. However, my preparation was not as disciplined as it should have been. Although I performed better than I did on the PSAT, my SAT score was significantly lower than I had anticipated. How could someone who is ranked second in his graduating class perform so poorly on the SAT? I would continue to ask myself questions of this nature until I finally met with Dr. Cohen.

Dr. Cohen was not pleased to hear that I used an undisciplined approach to preparing for the SAT. Surprisingly, Dr. Cohen told me that I would still be in contention for scholarship money. After seeing the puzzled look on my face, she emphasized that I had a good academic record, was the current SGA president, and came across well during face-to-face meetings.

Dr. Cohen and I continued to work closely for the remainder of the school year. She provided me advice as I applied to colleges. She also introduced me to various organizations that were offering recognitions and scholarship money. Due to her efforts, I competed for recognitions and scholarship money offered by organizations such as Rotary International, Alpha Phi Alpha Fraternity, Omega Psi Phi Fraternity, and several others. As I met persons affiliated with these organizations, it became clear that the members knew Dr. Cohen. As a high school senior, I remembered thinking that she knew how to work a room. She was personable, witty, professional, and politically astute. It was during this time that Dr. Cohen introduced me to networking. Dr. Cohen explained to me that sometimes who you know is as or more important than what you know. She also recommended that I consider joining a fraternity during my college years. After all, she and her husband were proud members of Alpha Kappa Alpha Sorority and Alpha Phi Alpha Fraternity, respectively. These sorority and fraternity affiliations had served them well over the years. In fact, Dr. Cohen would smile and make comments like "Membership has its advantages." Little did we know at the time that I would become a member of Alpha Phi Alpha during my sophomore year in college. Once again, Dr. Cohen was correct. My fraternal relationships have aided me in business and during personal crises.

Dr. Cohen played a key role in my selection of Savannah State College (now University) as my undergraduate institution. She also played a key role in helping me develop application packages and preparing letters of recommendation. Due to her tireless efforts, I was able to receive a Sarah Mills Hodge academic scholarship to Savannah State.

I graduated from high school in June 1985. However, my relationship with Dr. Cohen did not end at my high school commencement. During the past 25 years, Dr. Cohen has continued to serve as a mentor. However, I now consider her to be a friend and confidante as well.

As an undergraduate, I sought Dr. Cohen's advice on graduate schools. She and several others helped me to select Virginia Tech as the university that I would choose to attend for my master's of public administration degree, which I received in May 1990—approximately 1 year after receiving my undergraduate degree from Savannah State. Dr. Cohen was correct. I had much more to offer than a test score.

During my postgraduate years, Dr. Cohen has guided me in making key career decisions. In 1997, I decided to leave the U.S. General Accounting Office (now the U.S. Government Accountability Office) to pursue a consulting career. In January 1998, I joined the prestigious management and information technology consulting firm Booz Allen Hamilton, Inc. I have also worked for Deloitte Consulting and Stanley Associates. I now work for the MITRE Corporation. With each move, I sought and received Dr. Cohen's advice. She has always been there to lend a helping hand.

In March 2000, my wife had a miscarriage while pregnant with our first child and almost died. A small circle of family and friends helped us to bounce back from this painful episode. Dr. Cohen had a front row seat. If she was uncomfortable about our discussions, she never admitted it. Thanks to her advice, my wife and I did not give up on having a child. In February 2002, our son was born. I often think of how unfulfilled we would be had we decided to end our quest for having a child. Once again, Dr. Cohen was there to provide the correct advice.

Vince and his wife Cheri with Dr. Cohen in 2006

People who know me well say that I have lived a full life. These people also tell me that I have made wise decisions along the way. If they are correct, these decisions have been based, in large part, on advice that I have received from Dr. Eula Cohen—my high school guidance counselor, mentor, friend, and confidante.

7

Jennifer E. Fleming, PhD, PMP, IT Project Manager

"Mentoring is careful blend of approach and balance, particularly . . . sensitive to the recipient and challenging to the provider"
—Jennifer Fleming

Mentoring is an opportunity to extend oneself to others. This extension can manifest itself in a variety of settings—some personal and other professional. I have elected to share two perspectives of mentoring experiences in my life. The first experience describes the type of mentoring I received growing up and includes the types of interactions and observations that helped to shape and form my personality and perspectives. The second experience describes a professional mentoring relationship I shared with members of my team that demonstrates how I transferred my learning, skills, and experience to others to help them overcome challenges and adversity within their lives.

From my adolescent years, I am reminded of the mentoring relationship with my parents that provided me with a sense of nurturing and fostered excellence in academia. In my adolescent years, I was surrounded with a wealth of resources that provided me breadth and depth in scientific, sociological, and emotional knowledge. Education has always been an important part of my childhood and life. This was most likely attributed to the fact that I was a child of an educator. The pursuit of knowledge and academic excellence was fostered in a number of ways in our household.

Formal learning began as I accompanied my mother to work and assisted with the preparation of the libraries for each new school year. We organized books by the Dewey Decimal system, created media displays that featured caricatures that promoted reading and learning in animated and enticing settings, decorated the reading rooms, and reviewed the summer reading lists. I met teachers, librarians, principals, and administrators in a nontraditional manner that enabled me to see the importance of learning from their perspective and the passion, commitment, and sacrifice they made to create the environment and facilitate the process.

The structure of this exchange was dependent on the season of focus; during my school year, an expectation of excellence was present but rarely stated, as it was already understood that this dedication to academia would be upheld and maintained. In the summer, I was strongly encouraged to learn about relationships between individuals, families, and society vicariously through lengthy reading lists and social gatherings with friends and family members. And occasionally we discussed decision-making strategies and ways to ascertain motive and maturity in my interactions with people. Although I was young, the majority of my free time was spent in the presence of adults and elders who had a tremendous influence on my perspective and personality.

My father complemented and balanced this formal learning with social interactions in a different setting. My visits to West Florida (his hometown) to visit relatives exposed the city child to country living. I learned about farming, harvesting, food preservation, and extended family. We observed people preparing the field for planting, harvesting the crop, slaughtering and smoking meats, and preparing cannery. I also experienced an alternative form of religion, as most of my father's relatives were Southern Baptist, which was a sharp contrast from my Presbyterian upbringing. These interactions were a welcome interlude from the city routine and were often interspersed with other social gatherings or tailgate parties at sporting events. It is from these experiences that I learned the importance of balance and the need to extract one's self from the daily routine to renew and refresh.

I also observed a deep sense of connection and commitment to family and fraternal organization. My father's family experienced a horrific tragedy one day during one of our visits. It was an event of domestic violence that could have easily torn the family apart. Instead, they bound together and embraced the difficulty with love and compassion, and I have always admired them for that quality.

I recognize my parents as two of the most influential mentors in my life, as their guidance and actions shaped whom I have become. My success was most often measured by academic achievement in the form of a reward or title. The reward afforded them a form of acknowledgment of their transference of learning or the demonstration of a good deed. My commitment to the completion of a doctoral degree was in part dedicated to the tremendous and unspeakable personal sacrifice extended to provide an opportunity and environment for my success. Although the quantity and quality of my interactions with my parents differed significantly, their influence remains intact.

*   *   *

As a people manager, I am often tasked with the
responsibility of inspiring, guiding, assessing, and
rewarding resources. Most often these are company
resources, but occasionally there are contract resources.
During my tenure in the information technology industry, I
have directly and indirectly managed several resources,
three of whom were experiencing significant personal
trials. The following summarizes these experiences.

The first young lady will be called Sonja, and is a
talented and assertive young Hispanic lady. She was well-
known within her organization for being technically gifted,
having tremendous attention to detail, and delivering
performance. Unfortunately, she was equally known for
her assertiveness, feisty tongue, and revealing attire, and
Sonja had been overlooked for several job promotions. My
task was twofold: (1) to continue to cultivate the
professional spirit of this young lady and provide further
opportunities for her to demonstrate her capabilities and (2)
to refine her external attributes and help her tone down the
perceived abrasiveness of her presence within professional
settings. First, I worked to keep her in challenging
assignments that capitalized on her technical prowess and

oratorical skills. Second, I set up quarterly sessions with her to discuss professional etiquette and cultural differences. I began these sessions with simple conversations seeking to understand how things were going, but made certain we covered these topics in between the banter of checking in. In time, she began to moderate her attire, cite instances when she consciously held her peace, and speak proudly of her accomplishments and accolades from teammates.

The second young lady will be called Martha. My interactions with Martha were unique as we actually interviewed for the same job that I now hold. This was further complicated by the fact that after the promotion occurred, Martha was diagnosed with a life-threatening disease and was not expected to live for more than 6 months. In this scenario, I was tasked with helping a senior employee deal with a perceived failure and known mortality. I began by first giving Martha the space she needed to feel a sense of comfort with decisions that had been made and the personal calibration that was required. Martha initially decided to tell everyone of her personal challenge openly and did not conceal the severity of the situation. She later found that this vastly known knowledge was too overwhelming and she could not conduct work in an objective manner because people were paying too much attention to her needs rather than the job requirements. She worked for 1 or 2 months before leaving for short-term disability. During the initial phase, I offered some consultation when appropriate and shared some details of my experiences with the disease from my interactions with my mother and from Internet searches on support groups in the area. Martha embraced this personal challenge with remarkable resilience; her giftedness in artistic expression allowed her to make light of the treatment sessions and help the doctors and nurses with levity. The night before her radiation sessions, she drew pictures of cartoon characters on her body upside down and developed inspiring poems to help the other patients in the room to promote peace, love, and kindness. She kept others around her smiling regardless of the pain she felt internally, because she wanted others to win even if she would not. Our sessions were short, somber, and tearful, but full of open, honest discussion about life and those who share it. After we received notice of her final day, our entire team and organization visited her home and saw the many artistic works she had created during this journey. The home was full of paintings, sculpture, poems, and glasswork, all beautifully creative and explicative of her love of life and the people therein. She will forever remain in our hearts.

The last young lady was experiencing a challenge of domestic violence. This woman, who will be called Amy, was a young mother of two small children. She had ended a relationship with her children's father several years earlier and he was not happy with this situation. Amy had begun a new life with another gentleman who was well received by her family and children. The relationship angered their children's father and caused periodic inflammatory interactions during standard working hours. The stress of the situation and prior physical abuse had taken its toll on her self-esteem and physical health. I was tasked with helping Amy find help for the situation through the company human resources, maintain satisfactory performance at work, and improve her self-confidence and self-esteem. I provided her with a list of support services provided by the company; assigned her smaller, more manageable projects to help balance the work–life demands, and conducted biweekly check-in sessions to oversee performance and physical ability. I also gave her a copy of a popular little book titled *Who Moved My Cheese* as a lighthearted read to encourage her to think about developing a next-step plan for herself and her children, which became the impetus for her decision to seek legal and professional help to provide a safe shelter for her family.

8
Christopher L. Daniel, PMP, Principal, Regroup Partners International Consulting

"You've got to get to the stage in life where going for it is more important than winning or losing."
—Arthur Ashe

Mentoring is essential to professional and personal achievement. The ability to learn from someone that has gone before you is of utmost importance to the ongoing leading, learning, and sharing principles of total leadership. My passion lies in the synergy of mentorship. I believe an individual cannot ultimately enjoy the rewards of being a mentee unless he or she has been a mentor. I've served as mentor in several civic capacities as well as enterprise settings over the past 9 years. Each opportunity provided just as much time to learn as to lead. However, it wasn't until I signed a mentorship contract with Dr. McCollum that I began to see immeasurable results. This relationship came from a group leadership seminar that allowed me to develop a profound love for learning, growing, and developing into the leader I am now.

There are several characteristics that improve the quality of mentorship success, the most important being open communication. The ability to dialogue openly, give and receive constructive criticism, and develop a progress plan to keep moving is continuous. A mentor should not simply agree with a mentee's vision, but should critique the ideas and offer alternative perspectives and a plan of achievement. When I serve as a mentor, I use the model below:

$$A(S+K) + Goals = PBC => IR$$

Attitude (Skills and Knowledge) + Goals = Positive Behavioral Change that leads to Improved Results

The management by commitment (to change) approach, which is the same process I use when consulting, is essential to see real results in a short amount of time. The goal planning process is measured on a weekly basis with rewards, consequences, and growth. A new tool that has been introduced in my mentorship has been the use of executive journals (traditional or online). By jotting down important things on a daily basis, leaders can measure their effectiveness against life's challenges.

In my mentorships, success is measured much like effective organizations—consistently. By developing goals with the end in mind and working backward tactically, success is taken in smaller bites. Goal achievement works with momentum. Once a mentee sees the accomplishment of several smaller goals, the larger ones become more realistic. My mentorship goals are simple:

1. To enable a successful mentorship through goal accomplishment.
2. The mentee must serve as a mentor after the end of the mentorship period.

Mentorship is the tool that successful leaders use to advance. Mentorship completely changed my life. As a mentee, I transitioned from an employee to a thriving entrepreneur, certified project manager, board member, author, and mentor—in a short period of time. From a mentor's view, I continue to learn from the experiences, drive, and charisma of my mentees. The relationships formed through this process are lifelong and powerful enough to change the culture of global leadership.

9
Wava T. Johnson, Lean Six Sigma Training and Certification Program Manager

"Everyone is a prisoner of his own experiences. No one can eliminate prejudices—just recognize them."
—Edward R. Murrow

Mentor. A friend entrusted by Odysseus with the education of his son, Telemachus. The definition of mentor that appears in Merriam-Webster's dictionary begins as far back as the Trojan War. Merriam-Webster further defines mentor as "a close, trusted, experienced counselor or guide" (Merriam-Webster, 1993)." I view mentoring as a sharing of knowledge and agree with Aristotle (350 BCE), who stated, "All men by nature desire to know."

There is nothing more rewarding than experiencing a moment of learning. Simply put, we have those in our societal community who want to learn and seek out those who teach. We also have those in our community who want to learn, but have reached an impasse as a result of their environment and ultimately lose hope. Finally, we have those who choose to learn what is most relevant to their survival because the fear of experiencing something new is the result of not having someone who can lessen that fear. So many children and adults experience the fear of knowing. This is why I mentor.

It's tough to state when I started mentoring. I have spent most of my adult life serving my country in some capacity. In doing so, my development always included learning to develop someone should the day come when I would have to move on. So, it would be safe to say I have been mentoring in some capacity since I was 21—about 29 years of mentoring. I would say that I have been mentored all of my life.

Mentoring is hardly new or unfamiliar. Mentoring is one of the most traditional ways in which one generation communicates its experience and values to the next. We are all born with potential and a special gift. It is my argument that either we can encourage growth through nurturing or we can paralyze growth by providing the wrong nurturing or none at all. Someone has to model the behavior. Someone has to validate the curiosity within us. We all need mentors.

Throughout my experiences as a mentor, one thing always stood out—commitment. Both the mentor and the mentee must be committed to the mentoring relationship.

According to Rhodes (2002), mentors can influence their protégés' development in three important ways:

       * By enhancing social skills and emotional well-being.

       * By improving cognitive skills through dialogue and listening.

       * By serving as a role model and advocate.

Although I have mentored in various capacities, one that would best illustrate the mentor and mentee relationship would probably be in a professional or job-related environment. So, let's look at mentoring from the career development perspective.

Career development as it relates to mentoring is a process by which the mentor helps the mentee plan his or her career path. Additionally, career development encompasses career management and career planning. Researchers Milkovich and Boudreau (1997) noted that careers develop through the interaction of mentee choices to pursue their aspirations and organization choices to provide opportunities that advance organizational goals and objectives. Those career development areas that a mentor must influence are career planning activities and career management activities.

Career planning activities consist of the processes through which individual mentees identify and implement steps to attain career goals. For example, mentees should develop individual development plans. It is a requirement for me to review and update my individual development plans yearly. These plans should include an outline of broad developmental objectives based on a review of performance standards, past performance ratings, and career counseling sessions. So, who is responsible for ensuring that the aforementioned is accomplished? The mentor is responsible for ensuring that performance standards are set and met and mentoring sessions are productive.

The mentor also acts as a catalyst, sensitizing the mentee to the development planning process. This includes building an interpersonal relationship and fostering buy-in to the process. Career development promotes vertical and horizontal knowledge transfer throughout an organization.

Mentors assess the realism of the mentees' expressed objectives and perceived developmental needs to match an organization's goals and objectives. This process continues throughout the organizational life cycle and requires the mentor to follow up and update mentee plans.

One of the career management activities that mentors influence is the validation of mentees' information. How do you know or determine what your mentee may need or already have in his or her development toolkit? Validation of the toolkit provides the mentor with the information necessary to identify career development opportunities (job openings, training programs, rotational assignments, etc.) for mentees. The toolkit allows the mentor more clarity for guidance and enables the mentor to guide accordingly. Understanding the toolkit is very important to ensuring knowledge, skills, and abilities are current and will meet the needs of the future.

Human resource research has noted that work processes are increasingly driven by what employees (mentees) know. So, there is a direct link between knowledge and performance. Proper training of personnel provides a host of benefits such as enhancing performance and morale and reducing turnover (Roberts, 2002). The mentee depends on the mentor to identify skills that are lacking that preclude the mentee from being successful in meeting goals and objectives. Who can better identify these requirements than the mentor?

Today's leader has to be both a mentor and a coach. Coaching is the continuous effort to help mentees maximize their capabilities through personalized counseling and advice. The coaching process not only helps develop mentees to become familiar with business processes and expectations, but also motivates them to reach both individual and organizational goals.

Coaching is beneficial to mentees because it encourages them to discover their value and potential to the organization. Mentors who properly employ good coaching techniques build employee confidence, improve work habits, and increase productivity. According to Harkavy (2007), a good coaching leader is always moving and improving, sees who his or her people can become, is an improver, helps his or her players move from Point A to Point B, never accepts the status quo, is succinct and truthful, identifies gaps and gifts, inspires, sees the big picture and clarifies the steps necessary for success.

Coaching is a learning experience requiring a motivation to learn. Coaching provides an opportunity for mentors to use knowledge and skills. The process can be systematic and should not be limited to formal sessions.

Effective leaders use coaching at every opportunity possible. A major consideration of coaching is that it has to be conducted in a supportive environment, through clear communication, thus resulting in a mutual level of trust between the coach and the coached.

For many years, organizational leaders have used mentoring to enhance the potential of their employees. Leaders have to be cognizant of the tools available for their use that can assist them with the development of their subordinates, as well as their peers. Mentoring is a tool that has a proven track record of success.

Allen, Poteet, and Burroughs (1997) conducted research that indicates mentoring others may lead to greater job satisfaction, increased motivation, and the enhancement of the leadership skills of mentors. Their research further indicated that those who are mentored reap significant benefits, such as higher overall compensation, career development, and career satisfaction.

Mentoring programs within organizations are based on the concept that inexperienced employees more quickly acquire skills and knowledge that enhance their effectiveness and value if they learn from an experienced member of the organization. Mentoring is not only an aid to career advancement and promotion, but is also an excellent system for assisting an employee in developing other knowledge, skills and abilities. We all need mentoring in some capacity. The strategies covered provide a sound foundation for conducting mentoring at home, in schools, at work, and so forth. Individuals should have a sense of community and mentor someone to achieve their potential. The intrinsic benefits that will result might be surprising.

References

Allen, T. D., Poteet, M. L., & Burroughs, S. M. (1997). The mentor's perspective: A qualitative inquiry and future research agenda. *Journal of Vocational Behavior, 51,* 70–89.

Aristotle. (350 BCE). *Metaphysics by Aristotle* (Trans. W. D. Ross). Retrieved March 14, 2010, from http://classics.mit.edu/Aristotle/metaphysics.html

Baldwin, J. (1991). *The fire next time.* New York, NY: Random House.

Harkavy, D. (2007). *Becoming a coaching leader: The proven strategy for building your own team of champions.* Nashville, TN: Thomas Nelson.

Merriam-Webster. (1993). *Webster's third new international dictionary of the English language unabridged.* Springfield, MA: Author.

Milkovich, G. (1997). *Human resource management.*
    Boston, MA: Irwin McGraw-Hill.

Roberts, J. (2002). The policy was perfect. *Security
    Management, 46*(9) , 92-98.

10
Tony Camp, Counseling Intern/Educator

"People grow through experience if they meet life honestly and courageously. This is how character is built"
—Eleanor Roosevelt

Life has not been easy. At times, I have questioned whether I possessed the skills and competencies necessary to succeed in my field of study. Although this ride has not been as smooth as I thought it would be in the beginning, I am blessed to know that there has been one individual who has been available to guide me on my journey through school and life.

It was at Bowie State University where I met Dr. John W. Bryant. Dr. Bryant came to Bowie State University when I was in my sophomore year He earned his bachelor of science degree from Norfolk State University and his master of arts and doctoral degrees from Howard University. Dr. Bryant was a great mentor because he was often available when I had questions concerning courses to take to graduate, graduate school, or the challenges I was facing as a part of life. Dr. Bryant and I had an instant connection because we both enjoyed jazz, self-help books, observational learning, and the counseling field.

One experience I remember was when I was having difficulty deciding on the type of field of psychology as a focus for graduate school. At this time, it was suggested by our professors that students major in clinical psychology because it allowed students to do almost anything relating to psychology. Therefore, I had a talk with Dr. Bryant and he mentioned that obtaining a degree in clinical psychology would allow individuals to pursue any working position within the field of psychology, but the field is very competitive. Then, Dr. Bryant asked me about my future goals. The one thing I was sure about was that I wanted to receive a masters degree in psychology and later a doctoral degree. Also, I was sure that I did not want to leave the Washington, DC, area to go to school because my family and friends were here. Dr. Bryant encouraged me to look into the psychology programs at Howard University. I looked into the program, read its requirements and did some careful thinking. Two weeks later, I made the decision to apply to the master of arts in counseling psychology program at Howard University. When I informed Dr. Bryant of my decision to apply to the program, he was pleased and offered to write a recommendation. In May 2003, I received a letter of acceptance to the program. After I informed my parents of the acceptance letter, I informed Dr. Bryant and sent him a thank you card.

Dr. Bryant also played a role in my research interest. While at Bowie State University, I was struggling with the fear of public speaking and engaging in social situations. I went to Dr. Bryant's office and spoke with him about my fear and he encouraged me to read a book by Dale Carnegie called *How to Win Friends and Influence People*, which had helped him deal with his fear of public speaking. After reading the book, I learned to manage my fear of public speaking and social situations. As I was completing my research of the program at Howard University, I discovered that the graduates were required to complete a master's thesis. The topic I chose to explore was social anxiety among college students. When completing the study, I often thought about Dr. Bryant because he was the person who influenced me on this topic.

Dr. Bryant has helped me to prepare for presentations. One thing that Dr. Bryant told me was that people who enter the psychology field must be comfortable making presentations in front of an audience. Dr. Bryant encouraged me to rehearse presentations by standing in front of a mirror and presenting to family members. At times, I am still extremely anxious about making presentations in front of an audience, but I make sure I rehearse prior to the main event. The message from Dr. Bryant was especially helpful when it was time to present the results from my master's thesis. When I completed my thesis, I thought the most difficult portion of the process was presenting the results to my committee and other students. To prepare, I rehearsed the presentation of the results to my parents as Dr. Bryant had suggested, which helped to decrease my nervousness. I was still nervous about whether I would be able to answer the questions posed by my committee and fellow students. Later, Dr. Bryant reminded me that it would be impossible to answer all the questions posed by individuals concerning research results. Dr. Bryant suggested that when questions cannot be answered about research, you can recommend future research. The day I was presenting the results from my thesis, the situation was similar to what Dr. Bryant had told me concerning questions I would be asked by my committee. Once the question and answer session was completed, I felt a sense of relief because I did my best and followed the instructions that Dr. Bryant had given me. As a result, I passed the thesis defense stage and part of the success goes to Dr. Bryant for helping me through this phase toward graduation.

In addition, Dr. Bryant was the individual who taught me the importance of joining professional psychological organizations. One day, I was talking to him about the courses I was taking and he asked whether I was a part of any organizations. When I answered no, Dr. Bryant informed me of the importance of joining psychological organizations in order to network with others and be informed about current research in the field. Dr. Bryant also added that presenting work at conferences would provide an opportunity to meet people. One of my professors from George Mason University, where I am currently a doctoral student, had touched upon this subject in class just 2 days before. Following the advice of Dr. Bryant and my professor, I completed research on a number of organizations and decided to join the Association of Black Psychologists and the American Counseling Association. I am a member of these organizations and have attended their conferences. I really appreciate the recommendation that Dr. Bryant had given me because it has allowed me to network with others and understand current research.

Dr. Bryant was the type of mentor who always had confidence in my abilities. At times, I would question whether I had the skills necessary to succeed in the psychology field and Dr. Bryant has been there to guide me through the struggles. A few years ago, I was failing a statistics course and was feeling depressed because this was the first time in my education that I was in danger of failing a course. I spoke with Dr. Bryant and he encouraged me to study harder and to find a person from the class who could tutor me so I would not fail the course. He also added that he would be disappointed with me if I was removed from school for failing a course for which I didn't work hard. The disappointment on his face was enough to encourage me to do better. Once I stopped feeling depressed, I asked a classmate for help and started to put extra time into studying for the course. Dr. Bryant checked up on me often to see how I was doing in the course I was failing and to offer me some support. At the end of the semester, it was time to take the final for the course and I was under a lot of pressure to do well to pass the course. When I submitted the final, I discovered that I was the last person to finish. I learned that I had passed the final and would not fail the course. The confidence that Dr. Bryant had in me encouraged me to work hard and remain strong through my challenges with the course.

The success that I have experienced in school would not have been possible without Dr. Bryant. He has been there for me whenever I had questions about something, when I was feeling depressed because I was not doing well, or when I was nervous about speaking in public. It is very important for individuals to have someone in their life who has gone down the path they are traveling and is there to provide guidance along their journey. This is what it means to have a mentor.

11
Roberé Jock Brunson, Financial Services

"But if any provide not for his own, and specially for those of his own house, he hath denied the faith, and is worse than an infidel."
—1 Timothy 5:8 (King James Version)

Many times in our lives we encounter individuals who impact our lives in either a positive or negative manner. We have a tendency to embrace, follow, or strive to measure up to those who create a positive environment or positive growth relationship in our lives. One such person that came into my life was Stephen Smith (Chief).

Chief and I met shortly after September 11, 2001, when I reported for military duty at Dover Air Force Base in Dover, Delaware. I arrived in the squadron and began working on the day shift maintenance crew. I met then Master Sergeant Smith during a weekend work detail. As we talked and began to share our backgrounds, I noticed that Chief was a man of conviction and principles. I also noticed that although he was soft-spoken, he had complete authority and respect from many others regardless of rank. After the weekend detail concluded, I requested a transfer to Chief Smith's work shift, knowing that as a junior noncommissioned officer, I would be able to grow both professionally as well as personally under his leadership. Upon reporting for duty, Chief and I began a mentor–mentee relationship that has been mutually beneficial. For his dedication, he was able to see a young noncommissioned officer develop into a model for leadership and a contributing citizen for the betterment of the local community. As a result of my willingness to submit to and seek out a person of his integrity and character, I have become a role model for the value of mentor–mentee relationships. I learned that a person's knowledge, skills, and abilities are not just for his or her personal benefit, but are for the growth and benefit of others. If you are willing to give a portion of your time to the development of at least one other person, the compounded effect can change not only that person but also their community.

As Chief Smith and I worked together on the aircraft parking ramp, he would make quality suggestions or offer alternative views to some of our tasks much in the way a cowboy would prod a steer in the direction he knew it should go. He didn't tell me that my method was wrong or that I was wrong, he would just suggest a different method and then evaluate how I handled the advice. This technique proved very valuable to me in learning how to deal with adults who may have been doing something for many years yet never realizing that a better way existed. Instead of telling someone they are doing something the wrong way and my way is better, I learned to preserve egos and minimize conflicts by suggesting a different direction, which helps the person to learn from the experience as well as for a mutual respect to develop.

In the area of leadership, Chief taught me to always take care of your people. As you grow with both rank and responsibility, your first priority is to have buy-in from your people. The leader of the group is the person who sets the pace and expectations. If and when an opportunity arrives and you have a chance to reward your people, then do so. Your face doesn't have to be the one that is on the cover of the magazine. If you put the face of your subordinate out front, it allows him or her to build a degree of self-esteem that might otherwise not have developed. Chief Smith made sure to teach me to put my people in different environments that would expose them to experiences in life that might be outside of their comfort zones. If this means spending your personal finances to do it, then bless others with what you have been blessed with. The greater effect would create another opportunity to grow one more person who could in turn grow another person, thus continuing to compound the results. I saw evidence of this as I watched the number of people who would flock to Chief for advice in many areas. They knew from exposure or experience that he would give his honest advice with the intention to better their life.

When it came to community involvement, Chief Smith hardly went anywhere without me. He first introduced me to various people of influence in the surrounding area. He taught me that it was important to build key relationships with community leaders who could produce results and whom you could reach out to. If an event was to be held in the surrounding area and the opportunity arose to boost the image of the Air Force Reserve, he knew who and how many people he could assemble to make the mission happen. He showed me how important it was to make a big impact while leaving a small footprint. It wasn't the event but the impact on building relationships that was important. Whether it was military-related community projects or cultural projects, he would give of his time and resources so the next generation could experience a life-altering event. I carry that with me to this day. If you can rally key people and have them give of their time and influence, communities could develop goodwill ambassadors and be strengthened. Chief also taught me to tell my story, about where I came from and how I arrived at this point and then let them know where I am headed. Whether we were doing a seminar for children interested in working with aircraft or adults who just wanted to know what options they could expose their children to, Chief Smith would be able to reach out to the right people and get answers and create opportunities.

My time with Chief Stephen Smith, although short at just 3 years, has had and continues to have a great impact upon my life. I have come to understand that we are here so that others may be enhanced and uplifted and not just for ourselves to become great. Chief's investment of time in me will continue to expand his influence among others. The principles that he taught are a direct reflection of the U.S. Air Force's core values: Integrity First, Service Before Self, and Excellence in All You Do. Chief Smith's life is based on great integrity and sound principles. From the moment I met him and having had the privilege of working with him, I understood our lives are for the service of others so their lives may be enhanced. He taught me that if you are going to do something, give it your best and leave everything else to God's will.

12
Marilyn K. Simon, PhD, Professor of Education

"A mind once stretched by a new idea never regains its original shape"
—Oliver Wendell Holmes

Frustration, pressure, anxiety, and stress cause many doctoral-degree-seeking learners to abandon doctoral programs. Brown and Rudenstine (1992) estimated that over 40% of those who begin the process never graduate. Despite a dearth of comprehensive national statistics, the attrition rate in doctoral programs could be as high as 50% (Smallwood, 2004). Successfully completing a doctoral degree becomes even more difficult in a nontraditional, distance learning doctoral program where face-to-face meetings between mentors and mentees are infrequent and sometimes nonexistent.

In the early 1990s, I supervised doctoral students in nontraditional, distance learning programs. In the mid-1990s, I guided doctoral students. In the late 1990s, I advised doctoral students. Since 2000, I have been mentoring doctoral students. Although my compensation and job description have remained the same, my approach and worldview have evolved.

A supervisor is someone who manages, administers, and oversees a project. A guide is someone who directs, leads, and points others in a certain direction. An advisor is a consultant who makes recommendations. A mentor supervises, guides, and advises, but also serves as a trusted counselor and teacher. Mentoring is a committed relationship that includes a focus on developing the strengths and the capabilities of another person. The role of a mentor is akin to that of a mother.

As the mother of two extraordinary adult children, I see mentoring and mothering as similar activities. Some of my favorite quotes about mothering apply to mentoring:

- A mother [mentor] is not a person to lean on, but a person to make leaning unnecessary. — *Dorothy Canfield Fisher*

- A good mother [mentor] is like a quilt. She keeps her children warm but doesn't smother them. —*Anonymous*

- It is not what you do for your children [students] but what you have taught them to do for themselves that will make them successful. — *Ann Landers*

- A good mother [mentor] makes a long journey seem shorter. —*Unknown*

What has served my own children (mentees) well is my commitment to treat each child (mentee) as an individual, provide security, instill trust, offer tough love when necessary, and be their advocate. With both mothering and mentoring, I have learned that there is no script to follow, there is no one size fits all, and there are no guarantees that your efforts will be rewarded. However, by adhering to the three high Cs—competency, consistency, and caring—the chances of success increase exponentially.

Competency: *Those who dare to teach must never cease to learn. —Anderson (1980)*

Doctoral mentors need to be open to learning to enhance their mentorship. An effective doctoral mentor is a lifelong learner and remains knowledgeable in his or her field: knowledgeable about research methodologies, knowledgeable about the mentee's topic, knowledgeable about the doctoral process, and knowledgeable about scholarly writing. Attending professional meetings, reading professional journals, having a willingness to accept multiple perspectives, and participating in scholarly seminars and workshops helps the mentor ensure he or she has the competencies to meet the challenges of mentorship.

Consistency: *Successful people do ordinary things with extraordinary consistency.* —*Jon Gordon*

Completing a quality dissertation is wrought with road blocks. A dissertation must pass the *ROC bottom test* by being *researchable, original,* and *contributory.* This requires reviewing hundreds of scholarly manuscripts. As noted by Boote and Biele (2005), acquiring the skills and knowledge to be a scholar entails analyzing and synthesizing the research in a field of specialization, which is a prerequisite for increased methodological sophistication that ensures the usefulness of research.

Conducting meticulous and rigorous research that includes collecting, organizing, analyzing, and interpreting data requires hundreds, if not thousands, of hours of dedicated work. A doctoral mentor needs to guide his or her mentee on the path to success and prepare the mentee for challenges that arise but maintain a consistent and unfaltering faith that the mentee will persevere.

An effective mentor, like an effective mother, expects his or her mentees (children) to do well. This involves consistent communication, consistent cheerleading, consistent goal setting, and consistent guidance. The mentee (child) also needs to be consistently reminded to keep the destination in mind while enjoying the journey.

Caring: Mentees need to know a mentor cares before they care what the mentor knows. —Paraphrased by author

A caring mentor understands that *life happens* and that *a bend in the road is not the end of the road, unless you fail to make the turn.* There are days when nothing seems to be going well on the doctoral journey. This is the time when the mentor can provide an extra level of needed support. This could involve assisting in locating a document that will elucidate a complex concept, finding an alternative path for data obtainment, or simply lending a sympathetic ear. A mentee needs to know that the mentor is the mentee's advocate and is there to accompany him or her on the doctoral voyage. A caring mentor is sensitive to the needs of the mentee and generally recognizes when the mentee requires support, direct assistance, or independence.

I have had the honor and privilege of successfully mentoring over 100 doctoral students, and I have served on more than twice that number of doctoral committees. A successful doctoral mentorship is one in which the mentee completes his or her dissertation in a reasonable time frame, passes all academic reviews, and meets all university requirements for degree completion. Although each mentor–mentee relationship has been unique, two particularly stand out. What follows is a brief description of the mentees' dissertations and the process and relationship told primarily in the mentees' own words. The mentees are referred to by the first letter of their first names. I am Dr. M.

Back story 1: Dr. L's dissertation was a grounded theory study regarding the use of theater to initiate social change. Dr. L was an actress who had experienced life-changing events during her doctoral journey. These included the loss of her first husband, remarrying, and giving birth to two children. Dr. L had a prior mentor, Dr. B, whom she had worked with for 4 years before Dr. L requested that I take his place.

According to Dr. L: *My prior mentor–mentee relationship was confusing. Dr. B wanted me to conduct a semiological study. This type of study deals with the systems of meaning through which a culture is manifested and models aspects of human thought and action. I could not connect general semiotics to socially relevant theater and film as I knew it. This delayed my graduating by at least a year. It took me a while to figure out that there was no way I was going to write about anything I was not passionate about. It also took a while for me to figure out that a mentor was not my boss! Dr. M sensed that a grounded theory study was more in line with my research archetype and that methodology would enable me to renew my passion about my research. Dr. M understood that a mentor is someone that is there for you but that your dissertation is YOUR dissertation. We met face-to-face about a half dozen times, but I knew she was only a telephone call away. She also seemed to call at just the right time.*

Postscript Dr. L's dissertation won an excellence award from her university. The theatrical piece she wrote for her dissertation was performed in several theaters in Los Angeles and Chicago. Dr. L is now teaching theater.

Back story 2: Dr. P conducted a quasi-experimental study on a homework program targeted for low socioeconomic parents to assist their children. Dr. P and I met at a residency and we bonded immediately. Dr. P was a full-time instructor at a 4-year college, a mother of three young sons, and a mathematician who lacked confidence in her writing and research skills.

According to Dr. P: *What helped me most in the beginning was the conversation we had face-to-face in Arizona. I had a couple of ideas for research that I thought would work, and Dr. M discussed some ideas, and then told me to browse more topics that might help me come up with a topic I was passionate about. That was the key for me. I found that parental involvement was a major contributor to academic success, but in low socioeconomic households it was rare for a parent to provide support for a child's mathematics homework.*

The book that Dr. M wrote [Dissertation and Scholarly Research, Recipes for Success] *was a valuable resource. This solved a lot of the "what's next" and "how to" questions for me. In the last stages of my dissertation process, Dr. M sensed that I needed a more left-brain, analytical approach to this process. She outlined that I had 17 more things to do, and I just went down the list and did them. The last 2 months we had daily contact and sometimes communicated several times a day. I always felt*

that Dr. M was there for me and truly cared about my
success.

Postscript Dr. P's dissertation won an educational award in the state of Arkansas. A program based on her dissertation was adapted throughout Arkansas.

Conclusion

Being a doctoral mentor, like being a mother, encompasses a complex set of issues with numerous interrelated variables that prevent a one-size-fits-all approach. Good mentorship, like good mothering, involves sensitivity and an intuitive understanding of when the child or mentee requires support, direct assistance, or independence, and the wisdom to know how each is to be applied.

References

Anderson, J. (1988). Cognitive styles and multicultural populations. *Journal of Teacher Education, 39*, 2-9.

Boote, D. N., & Beile, P. (2005) Scholars before researchers: On the centrality of the dissertation literature review in research preparation. *Educational Researcher, 34*(6), 3-15.

Brown, W. G., & Rudenstine, N. L. (1992). *In pursuit of the PhD.* Princeton, NJ: Princeton University Press.

Simon, M. (2010). *Dissertation and scholarly research: Recipes for success* (2nd ed.). Del Mar, CA: Worldpress.

Smallwood, S. (2004). Doctor dropout. *The Chronicle of Higher Education, 50,* A10.

13

Richard T. Brown, Jr., Senior Network Engineer/Site Manager

"You can have everything in life you want, if you will just help enough other people get what they want"
—*Zig Ziglar*

The first mentor who made any type of impact in my life is my father. My father and I have a very special relationship. It took me long time to realize how fortunate I was. It was not until I graduated from high school that I realized that none of my close friends were raised by their mother and father. Several of my friends did not have the opportunity to have a father in their life to teach them the lessons of life. I am blessed to have a father who was able to teach me the difference between right and wrong. I am blessed to have a father who was able to teach me to think before I act and to think about the consequences of those actions. At the time, I did not realize what my father was doing for me. I thought he was being a drill sergeant. I regularly felt that he treated me like one of the recruits he used to train when he was in the U.S. Army. Now I realize that my father was competent and confident that what he was doing was the right thing. My father was able to guide my siblings and me on many issues. I am not sure if he ever thought of himself as the best role model for us. To me, he was. He instilled his morals and values in me and gave me the necessary tools that all men should have. He also challenged me to be a better man than he could be. Many of the lessons I learned, I learned from my father. I did not have to search for mentors in the neighborhood or school, because I had one at home. Although my father and I do things differently, who I am today is a direct result of his guidance. He was always quick to tell me to do things better than he did in the past and not to make the same mistakes. For example, my father was raised on the eastern shore of Maryland and did not have the opportunity to attend the best schools. He was an exceptional athlete. He excelled in every sport he participated in, but always wished he had the opportunity to go to college. There was no such opportunity because he was drafted into the U.S. Army. Soon after, my father was married with children on the way. He made education a priority for me and my siblings. The skills he learned playing sports and from the military made him an excellent mentor. No matter how good any of us were at sports, if we did not perform in the classroom we were not allowed to perform on the field or court. This passion for education is the reason I am a lifelong learner to this day. This is just one example of how he wanted us to have the opportunities that he did not have.

My father was an influential mentor because he realized the importance of relationships within the family. He learned from his father that a stable relationship and marriage is the key to success. This foundation was built on having a happy home and striving to do an admirable job parenting. I strive to continue the same cycle with my family. My father was responsible for helping me succeed in life. My father is my guide when I have questions about marriage or raising a family. I am able to provide for my family because my father provided me with the tools to do so. My father continues to teach me to this day. He reminds me that no matter how smart I get or how much I accomplish, I will still need a mentor and he will always be there for me. I will always love my father for that!

TSgt Jackie Clarke

The next mentor that I encountered was technical sergeant (TSgt) Jackie Clarke. He was my first supervisor when I joined the U.S. Air Force. TSgt Clarke's philosophy was that none of us can make our way through the military, or life for that matter, without the advice and examples of others. For me, TSgt Clarke was more than a supervisor—he was my mentor. He was able to counsel and advise me on issues that have helped me professionally, emotionally, and spiritually. He was an ardent listener, which made him a strong leader. He was willing to mentor anyone who wanted to learn. No one was more eager to learn than I was. He was the type of leader who thoughtfully mentored me. He would only remind me to listen and pass on what I have learned to younger troops. His mentoring philosophy has helped me in so many ways. He helped me succeed in the military and my career outside of the military. He taught me the value of taking and giving advice and wise counsel. He taught me the value of taking the time to share ideas and experiences with others. What he taught me was the core competencies on which military leadership is founded. TSgt Clarke helped me realize that I made a decision to serve my country and that in doing so I have a professional responsibility to maintain while I wear a military uniform.

TSgt Clarke ensured that I was well-rounded and competent to meet my current and future military requirements. Having him as a mentor helped my professional development tremendously and gave me the skills to handle any increase in job responsibility. He taught me how to be a supervisor. He taught me to take care of the people around me. I learned quickly that in order to be successful it was necessary to take care of my colleagues and subordinates. I learned to make myself available to anyone who needed me and to provide an atmosphere that welcomes discussions and open dialogue. It took me a long time to realize that time is a valuable commodity and that I need to be willing to provide it when needed. TSgt Clarke also served as my checkpoint. He helped me develop provoking and stimulating thoughts. These thoughts led to ideas, visions, and goals, which have helped me become the man that I am today. As I emulated him, I found myself becoming a mentor and in a position to steer and guide subordinates. Through his example, I found myself becoming the guide to others on how to conduct themselves. Having a mentor and serving as a mentor was my stepping stone to becoming a leader. I was always easily motivated. All it took for me was to experience the care and concern from TSgt Clarke for my well-being and development. Thank you TSgt Clarke!

Dr. Walter McCollum

The last mentor I would like to talk about is my faculty mentor, Dr. Walter McCollum. When I began my

PhD journey 1.5 years ago, I really did not know what to expect. I was blessed to get, as the instructor of my first class, a man who is now my faculty mentor and friend. Dr. McCollum taught my very first class at Walden University and prepared me for an experience of a lifetime. Although I did not receive the grade that I strived for in that class, I did receive so much more. I reached out to Dr. McCollum after reading his class biography because we both shared a military background and live not too far from each other. From the very beginning, Dr. McCollum was willing to listen. He also gave me some excellent advice. I had the pleasure of meeting Dr. McCollum for the first time at my first residency, which was an enlightening experience as well. Shortly thereafter, Dr. McCollum became my faculty mentor and immediately made an impact on my journey. As a mentor, Dr. McCollum has a wealth of career experience and is willing to share that knowledge. Dr. McCollum is preparing me for PhD life after graduation. He requires more from me than other faculty mentors. I am being prepared by giving presentations to colleagues, writing additional papers, and attending conferences for professional organizations.

I have been told on numerous occasions by several faculty mentors that the relationship with your mentor is of crucial importance. I have been blessed to have a mentor like Dr. McCollum who is always willing to give emotional and moral encouragement. He is also very accessible. Dr. McCollum is available to me by phone, e-mail, or meetings when his schedule permits. As a mentor, Dr. McCollum has a formula in place that allows him to spend his time and energy to enhance educational development. I am excited about learning from faculty and other students and applying that knowledge into my own plans to bring about social change. Dr. McCollum sets high academic standards for himself and each of his students. As a result, I have been able to exceed the expectations of my teachers and myself. Although this is a process that one must go through in order to graduate, it is an enjoyable one for me. I have fully submerged myself into the Walden process because of the relationship that I have with Dr. McCollum. I enjoy working with Dr. McCollum. My intuition tells me that the feeling is mutual. Dr. McCollum is always there for support and never has a negative thing to say.

Dr. McCollum has given me a different perspective on mentoring. The success of our relationship is evident because all parties involved recognize the value of networking and maintaining relationships throughout our professional career. The gratitude I have for attending

Walden and having Dr. McCollum as a mentor is immeasurable. Dr. McCollum has taught me what it takes to succeed at this level. Also he has shown me his techniques to get the most out of my learning experience. He has also introduced me to faculty and other students to get connected to those in other arenas. I have yet to experience any of the frustrations that some of my colleagues with different faculty mentors are currently experiencing. Dr. McCollum's insight and knowledge of both the university and the industry has spared me a great deal of stress that is commonly felt by other students. As a mentor, Dr. McCollum demonstrates and upholds higher values and ethics aside from Walden that inspire me to try to do the same. At this point, I consider our relationship to be a two-way street with both sides being able to take advantage of what the other has to offer. This behavior causes me to be more proactive in my own mentoring relationships that I maintain with colleagues. My life has been changed drastically by the people that I have met and the professional organizations that I have joined. Since starting this journey at Walden, my career has catapulted tremendously. I thank the Lord every day for bringing me this far and introducing me to Dr. McCollum. Thanks Doc!

14
Gregory Campbell, Federal Law Enforcement Executive

"A life is not important except in the impact it has on other lives."
—Jackie Robinson

Growing up in Compton, California, life offered very little opportunity for a young African American boy, especially when it came to recognizing the importance of making an investment. However, as I got older, I learned that making an investment over time would pay off. What I did not understand in my early years was how my decisions would be influenced by the deposits others made into my account. Today, I recognize that the deposits made were not monetary, but were lessons, advice, experiences, and mentorship.

This is my story, a life forever changed by the investments of my father, football coaches, pastor, and college professor. Each of these individuals played an essential part in my discernible shift of momentum from humble beginnings to success, all because they cared to make a difference by making a willful deposit into my account called life.

The Power of Influence

My father, Gregory Campbell Sr., made the foundational deposit into my life by teaching me self-worth, work ethic, and the importance of education. Like many kids growing up in the inner city, the negative influences of gangs, drugs, jail, and death dominated my surroundings. However, my father taught me self-worth by challenging me not to allow my environment to dictate my future, but to believe that I could accomplish anything my heart desired. As a kid, I remember him telling me that I could be "Dr. Campbell." My father passed away in 2004 from lung cancer, but his words still live in my heart and are a source of motivation as I pursue my dream of becoming Dr. Campbell.

Additionally, my father taught me the importance of work ethic by instilling in me the value of working for things that I wanted. For example, he refused to buy my brother and me brand name shoes, such as Nike or Adidas. He would provide us enough money to buy shoes from a local shoe store and encouraged us to earn additional money if we wanted to purchase brand name items. As a result, I recall pushing a lawn mower up and down my block asking neighbors if they wanted their lawns cut for

$10.00. My father's principles of work helped me develop the confidence to ask the local gardner and milkman for an opportunity to work with them. This principle made it easier for me to obtain a number of jobs as a teenager and now guides my leadership behavior as a law enforcement executive.

The power of education was one of the most important investments my father made into my life. First, he taught me that education was a privilege that I could not afford to waste. As a young athlete with dreams of playing football for the University of Southern California, my father always taught me that my education came first and sports second. For instance, he would give me five dollars for every touchdown I scored, but he would give me ten dollars for each "A" I earned on my report card. My father's encouragement and discipline helped me become the first person in my family to earn a college degree.

My football coaches invested in my life by teaching me the importance of perseverance and teamwork. Like many inner-city youth, sports became my buffer or escape from the negative influences of my environment. As a kid, I played Pop Warner football for the Carson Cowboys under the leadership of Coaches Brown, Moore, and Reed, who were all in their late 40s or 50s. What amazes me to this day is that Coaches Brown and Moore did not have kids on the team, but cared enough for a group of young boys to invest their time and talent. Every year, the first couple of weeks of practice were dedicated to physical conditioning. I recall my coaches screaming that our hard work and perseverance during the 2 weeks of conditioning would pay off on the field. When exercises became tough and I wanted to quit, I recall them yelling, "Life is not easy, if you want something, you have to work for it. Persevere and never quit!" As a result, I have tried to apply what I learned on the football field to life as a college student, father, husband, mentor, and leader.

The power of teamwork was another important principle I learned from my coaches. Most of the boys played together for approximately 4 years and later into high school. First, Coaches Moore, Brown, and Reed taught me that I could accomplish more on the field by working as a team than by relying on individual skills. Second, they would often say that teamwork produces victories and our record, in which we only lost one game each season for 3 consecutive years, proved that. Teamwork has played a significant role in my leadership style, work performance, and mentoring.

Life Lessons as a Mentee

Dr. Samuel Huddleston has made substantial investments into my life as a mentor. He has helped me to grow in many areas of my life, especially by teaching me the power of relationships and accountability. It is my belief that you must give in order to reap the benefits of receiving life's blessings. Mentorship requires just that. Dr. Huddleston taught me how to treat people and most importantly how to serve. First, he demonstrated the power of relationships by serving and loving people wherever he went. For example, whether he was at the local coffee shop, restaurant, school, or prison, he treated people with dignity and respect. Dr. Huddleston has the gift of making anyone he engaged in conversation feel as if they are the most important person at that moment.

Dr. Huddleston believed that a person's choice of relationships could affect personal success. For instance, he would say, "If you hang around dogs, you might get fleas." I learned by watching Dr. Huddleston that some people collect coins, stamps, or cars, but it is important as a leader to learn to collect people. Dr. Huddleston and I would generally have our mentoring sessions at a local coffee shop or at his office, but on one occasion, he asked me to meet him at the Vallejo harbor. At the harbor, we boarded the yacht of our friend Dan Gordon and proceeded out into the water for our session. The lesson for that day was that you do not have to own a yacht, you just have to know someone who does. In my home, at my church, and on my job, I work at being a servant leader every day.

Dr. Walter McCollum has also invested in my life through his demonstration of true servant leadership. By his actions, he has taught me that a mentor should be personable, ingenious, genuine, generous, and inspiring. As a Walden University mentee of Dr. McCollum, I have watched him demonstrate excellence in mentoring and teaching by developing a peer–mentor program, conducting social dinners for students, Library of Congress research sessions, biweekly student presentations via teleconference, and graduation dinners for outgoing students. Dr. McCollum leads by example while impacting social change. Dr. McCollum lives a life that exemplifies leadership and his actions can be summed up in the words of Maxwell (2005), who stated, "Leaders need to be what they want to see" (p. 243). He is a leader, teacher, mentor, scholar-practitioner, social change agent, and motivator who has taught me the importance of paying it forward.

What Mentors Should Consider

Before becoming a mentor, it is important to consider three concepts. First, you must consider whether the person you are mentoring is teachable and worthy of the investment. Do they possess the capacity to learn and share their learning lessons with others? Call it intuition or just a gut feeling, but I knew my 17-year-old mentee, Khris Miller, was someone special. I was in charge of my church youth program and I did not have a worship leader, but desired to have music as a part of our service. I knew Khris was a young man who was not just content with just listening to music, but wanted to serve in the music ministry. In the beginning, Khris learned how to play the guitar to assist me in youth ministry and in 2008, he went on to graduate from one of the top music schools in the country, Berklee College. When someone is provided an opportunity, he or she must make the best out of it. This was the case with Khris Miller.

Second, you have to consider the mentee's experience. This is vital to developing a successful relationship. Mentoring requires a give and take relationship where both parties benefit from the investment. Lastly, you must envision the outcome of this investment.

Just as my father was my most important mentor, one of my most important mentees is my son, Jonathan. At the tender age of 11, Jonathan is already a talented football player, but he is also an excellent student. Jonathan often talks about being a professional football player, but he also believes that he will be Dr. Campbell someday. Without vision and goal setting, a ship will move blindly through dark cold waters without direction.

Inculcated within these three concepts are three phases of mentoring. The three phases of mentorship have become a structured process that has helped me become a better servant leader. They involve relationships, objectives, and accountability. Similar to developing a business plan, you must ascertain the relationship between the investor (mentor) and the account holder (mentee).

Relationships

Phase 1 requires trust and respect between the investor and the account holder. The mentee must believe and trust that the mentor is honest and truthful and maintains a position of credibility. It is difficult to maintain a healthy mentoring relationship when the elements of this phase are violated.

Objectives

Phase 2 mandates the importance of having objectives in the relationship. For example, if you set the objectives clearly at the onset of the investment, then it will provide structure in the relationship. Objectives outline the guidelines and boundaries between the investor and the account holder.

Accountability

Phase 3 requires the mentee to understand he or she is accountable to the mentor and must value the mentor's time, experience, and advice. In the final analysis, the mentee must take ownership of his or her personal and professional development. What the account holder earns from the investment must be reinvested in others!

I recognize that my father, football coaches, pastor, and college professor were instrumental in changing my direction from the predictable to the possible. For that, I am eternally grateful and feel blessed to share my experiences with you.

Reference

Maxwell, J. C. (2005). *The 360° leader: Developing your influence from anywhere in the organization.* Nashville, TN: Thomas Nelson.

15
Phillip D. Jackson, Reverend

"Life is understood looking backwards, but must be lived looking forward."
—Soren Kiekegaard

I have been mentoring returning citizens (men returning to their community after being incarcerated) for the past 4 years. I work for a nonprofit organization called the Reintegrated Alternative Personal Program (RAPP). My involvement with mentoring the aforementioned demographic resulted from teaching life skills classes in the District of Columbia correctional facility. I realized while teaching life skills that many of the men needed someone to facilitate the process of gaining the necessary life skills to move forward in life after being incarcerated. The highlight for me was the openness and honesty of these men to admit and request the need for assistance in getting started. Many of them were doing something they had never done before. For instance, some were establishing bank accounts for the first time in their life; most of them discovered how to engage into positive conversation and relationships with their families, communities, coworkers, and even their employers, and others learned to foster

143

partnerships with their parole or probation officers instead of an adversarial relationship. This began with teaching a life skills class and trickled down to developing a passion to give advice, coach, and provide these men with wise counsel. Presently, I mentor five adult African American males ranging in age from 45 to 47.

I believe the primary characteristic of mentoring is developing an atmosphere of truth and trust. This is done by defining truth and distinguishing its consequences from living a life of untruth. Since the mentees spend most of their time in a group with one of them as the leader, the mentor's responsibility is to guide most of the work and discussions done by the mentees. My sole responsibility is to facilitate the group and not dominate it. Each week the mentor provides one-on-one mentoring with each mentee to develop and establish commitment and trust and to cultivate the mentor–mentee relationship.

My program has two main goals, one is to teach cognitive skills and emotional intelligence and the other is to confront distorted thinking and improve self-esteem. If cognitive restructuring is to alter distorted thinking, then cognitive structuring is to validate and affirm positive or correct thinking. The model is a behavioral science method designed to show mentees how to overcome life's problems and be more successful. This is accomplished in part by assisting mentees to correct their distorted thinking (restructuring) while validating their correct thinking. The mentoring program is self-reflective and challenging. It involves a great deal of self-evaluation and internalization. In many cases, the mentees will learn the truth about themselves for the first time in their lives and will learn that they are much better people than they think they are. The program is designed to force the mentees outside of their comfort zone, where a positive change can take place. This is not a scared straight or threatening approach, but an approach that involves an increase in self-esteem, healing, and learning approach. Many studies have shown that an increase in self-esteem directly correlates to a person's ability and desire to improve in life. The group sessions are 12 sessions that meet once a week for 3 hours.

The goals of our mentorship are as follows:

- Mentor develops trust by being firm, fair, and caring, which ultimately allows the mentee to be more willing to listen.
- Mentor creates an atmosphere of excitement about the mutual adventure in self improvement.
- Mentor shares his own experience and input.
- Mentees complete class objectives.

- Mentees review and sign agreements.
- Mentees are acquainted with the motto and pledge.
- Mentees understand the focus of self-improvement.
- Group leaders understand the importance of small group leaders.
- Mentees understand the importance of personal reports in setting the mood of the class.

The success of the program is measured by pre- and posttesting. Test scores are generally low in the beginning, but most mentees show an increase of 60% to 70% between the pre- and the posttest.

The impact and outcomes of the mentorship program have a profound effect and are a life altering experience for both the mentee and the mentor. Although I have conducted many of these group sessions, I am still amazed and perplexed about the impact and outcomes that these sessions played in the lives of the men I have encountered. Many of these men have graduated and gone on to do exceedingly well in life considering their extensive criminal backgrounds. They regularly stop by or call just to let me know of their career and personal accomplishments, which I find rewarding and refreshing. The five men I am presently mentoring are all doing extremely well.

16
Vernotto McMillan, PhD, Aerospace Engineer

"In order to succeed, your desire for success should be greater than your fear of failure"
—*Bill Cosby*

Since the early stages of scientific management (i.e., Fredrick Taylor), researchers have developed, documented, tested, and institutionalized many different leadership styles. Leadership is the process of exercising influence from a position of formal authority in an organization, thereby getting an employee to do what the leader wants (Hunt, Osborn, & Schermerhorn, 1994). In lay terms, leadership is the ability to get people to want to do what needs to be done. Leaders use a purpose story to gain buy-in and commitment from their followers and employees. The talent and drive of the workforce is the key to an organization's success, and most scholars believe true leaders engender an effective use of power through high concern for people and high concern for production or team supervisory style (Desivilya, Lidogoster, & Somech, 2009).

Mentoring is an essential part of leadership. Without it, both leaders and subordinates are doomed to failure. My relationship with mentoring and my passion for it began in 1991 when I was detailed to a 2-year project in the Washington, DC, metropolitan area at the headquarters of a government agency. My direct supervisor was a high-ranking associate administrator and he introduced me to mentoring by serving as my first mentor. He instilled tremendous confidence in me by placing me in charge of controversial failure investigations of spacecraft vehicles and programs. During that period, I was a technical specialist/engineer with little leadership, oral presentation, and writing experience. Initially I was terrified at the level of responsibility that was assigned to me, but my mentor practiced management by walking around and provided me guidance, training, and the programmatic support I felt was necessary to meet my objectives (i.e., ability to travel to the site when needed). From this experience I grew more confident in my abilities and upon returning to my permanent work center location in the Southeastern region of the United States I became a fan of the use of mentorship in developing people. Over the years, I have attempted to use my personal experience in Washington to help me lead and mentor subordinates whom I have had the pleasure of working with. Assessing my experience, I identified a set of attributes that I have used in my mentoring activities:

* Confidence

* Guidance

* Personal improvement opportunities

* Obtainable goals

* Checkpoints

* Metrics

In this chapter, I would like to share a brief story of one mentee who I have worked with. I will refer to the mentee as Caroline. My relationship with Caroline began as a supervisor–subordinate relationship and lasted for more than 10 years. Today, I no longer work with her, but have watched her career expand from a distance.

Caroline was in her 40s when she began working with me in the Technology Program Office in the late 1990s. Her background consisted of software engineering development. One of the many missions of this office was the release of agency-developed software to the private sector or other public sector agencies. In my early years as deputy director of the Program Office, I was in charge of ensuring that the various mission objectives of the organization were met. This meant the employees performing the task had to be equipped with the right skills, tools, funding, and mentoring support to complete the task. Caroline was new to her job as the agency/center software release authority. She was tasked with not only managing the release of aency-developed software, but also developing a new streamlined software release process that would be used for the release of all agency-developed software. This had to be done while continuing to use the antiquated and cumbersome process that was already in place. The office received an average of 25-30 software release requests per week. Using the old process, only a fraction of the requests were getting released appropriately and timely. Delays in the release of various software codes led to schedule slippage in the projects and programs desiring to use the software. This was prompting some individuals in the software community to illegally release codes that had not been through the agency's release process. These acts were in direct violation of the agency's directive on software release.

Caroline was of Asian descent and her English accent was difficult for many of the software engineers in the technical organizations to understand. The language barrier, combined with the cumbersome process, created a difficult relationship leading to a compliance problem.

It was clear to me that Caroline was extremely intelligent and possessed a working-level knowledge of software code development. However, her lack of ability to verbally communicate effectively was an obstacle to her potential success as software release authority. Also, her lack of experience in developing an organizational work process was hindering her ability to make progress. During her first performance planning session I outlined a set of goals that would need to be achieved in order to move her in a positive direction toward task success. I tasked her to first outline or benchmark the current process so the steps could be identified and assessed. Next, her task was to research the agency requirements for software release to differentiate between what was currently done and what was required. Third, she was tasked with talking with the customers on both sides (i.e., internal and external), which includes the actual software engineers in the various organizations and the organizations that were applying for use of the software. This would provide her a perspective of their needs and the issues they were facing. Equipped with this knowledge, a new streamlined process could begin to take shape. She would need to be able to actively communicate the steps being taken and the potential progress of the new process to the entire community. Therefore, personal training opportunities were identified and approved. Within weeks, her oral communication skills were improving. More important, her confidence had greatly improved to the point where she was adding to her goals and felt a sense of ownership. Within 9 months, Caroline was at the self-actualization stage of Maslow's hierarchy of needs.

The six attributes previously identified were as follows:

* Guidance (Outline the steps and potential benefits of the steps to Caroline): (a) Keeping the subordinate directly focused on the task and outcomes and not allowing them to focus on negatives or failure and (b) helping them control their emotions and understand that reactions and disagreements by others in the technical community are not personal and should be viewed as steps toward progress.

* Personal improvement: As a leader I was able to assist and approve her involvement in Toastmasters International during and after work hours. Oral presentation training during work hours was imperative. Developing effective charts and delivering effective oral briefings was the goal. This was followed with daily speaking opportunities. Caroline was tasked with performing in-reach and outreach. She was tasked with delivering 15-minute briefings at all of the organizations.

She also attended technical staff meetings throughout the agency and delivered 5- to 10-minute briefings weekly. Her ability to communicate improved with each presentation.

* Obtainable goals (Small steps followed by incrementally larger steps): Mentorship goals include whether the employee is able to take control of the task. Does the need for supervisory input decrease over time? Is the subordinate now adding additional tasks and goals based on their foresight to improve the process? In short, situational leadership was used with Caroline. The situational leadership theory is defined by effectively integrating the task behavior of the employee and the relationship behavior of the manager (Blanchard, Hersey, & Johnson, 2008). The maturity or readiness level of followers, along with a leader's ability to adjust to the situation, is imperative. Readiness is the extent to which people have the ability and willingness to accomplish a specific task (Blanchard et al., 2008). As Caroline's skills and confidence improved, the amount of time invested in mentoring was decreased.

* Confidence (The subordinate needs to know the leadership has confidence in them and why): (a) always

instilling confidence in subordinates and letting them know that management both trusts and supports them to get the job done and (b) having the subordinate discuss weekly activities in 3-minute sound bites in the staff meeting.

* Checkpoints (Management by walking around): Perform daily tag-ups initially to see how things are going, followed by weekly tag-ups. Listen to the employee. Understand body language.

* Metrics (Measure success): Using a project management approach, assess the efforts to see if milestones have been met (i.e., complete outline of current process, complete draft of the new process, complete at least two organizational briefings per week, and gain approvals from management to execute the new process). How is the process working? Is there an improvement in the number of software releases on a weekly, monthly, or annual basis? Have we eliminated the illegal releases?

In summary, within a 2-year period, the organization was recognized for its metrics with respect to software release and Caroline was soon asked to lead the agency software release team, which consisted of all software release authorities from other center locations. Over time, her responsibilities continued to grow and her career continued on a positive track. As the organizational leader, I benefited from the success of the process improvement, but my most treasured accolade was the personal knowledge and experience of helping to nurture a talented individual to reach her potential through mentoring.

References

Blanchard, K., Hersey, P., & Johnson, D. (2008). *Management of organizational behavior: Leading human resources* (9th ed.). Upper Saddle River, NJ: Pearson, Prentice Hall.

Desivilya, H., Lidogoster, H., & Somech, A. (2009). Team conflict management and team effectiveness: The effects of task interdependence and team identification. *Journal of Organizational Behavior, 30,* 359-378.

Hunt, J., Osborn, R., & Schermerhorn, J. (1994). Managing organizational behavior (5th ed.). New York, NY: Wiley.

17
Cornellis K. Ramey, Pastor

"Never retreat in the face of difficulties. Advance as conditions permit. If conditions don't permit, create those conditions."
—*John C. Maxwell*

"The year is 1941, Marriott Chairman and President J.W. Marriott, Jr. is nine years old, the United States is about to enter Word War II, the Edsel is going to be the car of the future, and Willie Ramey begins working for Hot Shoppes in Washington, D.C." So reads the article published in *Marriott World* to commemorate my father's 50th year anniversary with the corporation in September 1991. I attended the function in my military dress blues as a token to his influence at home.

Fast forward to October 2010, and I have just turned 49, my father has been dead 5 years last month, and I have an opportunity to try to capture the essence of his impact upon my life. Amazingly, as most folks can attest to, it seems time has flown since that day in September 1991. This month I am celebrating my fourth year as a pastor, second year as an ordained minister (yes, one can pastor before ordination, but you cannot marry, bury, or handle the sacraments), 10 years since retiring after 21 years of honorable military service, 10 years ongoing security consultancy supporting intelligence and military missions, and 16 years removed from graduating with a master's of science degree in administration with an emphasis in operations research.

None of those things had been accomplished by that September 1991 celebration, but the source to ensure they all would be completed was receiving the accolades that day—Willie Ramey—my father, best friend, and biggest fan. At 49, I am reflecting upon what my father provided me. I will frame my reflection in line with my commitment, as an ordained minister, to the preaching of the gospel.

When I think of my father, I think of image and likeness. So, what are the four things God and my father accomplished? From this point forward, I will focus upon my father and my life; God and His legacy is for another time. My father did the following four things: (1) He provided for me, (2) he protected me, (3) he progressed me, and (4) he promoted me. The context in which he accomplished these four things was as a father of our family (wife and five children). In providing for his family, my father worked every day and during some periods he would work a part-time job as well. While working every day, his leadership and affection provided the protection all family units need. Although we did not have a sit-down dinner as a family every night, we had dinner every night— because my father protected us financially, emotionally, and physically, ensuring we had a roof over our heads, heat, lights, running water, and all the food the cupboard could sustain. This lifestyle allowed all of us to progress in life. We had the continuity of family, day-by-day, which allowed us to be in the moment, seasons, and eras of our lives according to our given ages. Having this day-to-day continuity gave us a healthy sense of innocence as well, protecting us from many of the harsh realities that life can impose from several veins, such as poverty, crime, and homelessness.

We did not grow up in a perfect world; we grew up protected in an imperfect world. Because we were protected, it allowed us to have a decent balance of emotions through all the phases of our lives and thereby put us in position to seize opportunities and promotions. Personally, I excelled in sports and even came on TV playing in and being on the winning team of a Marriott-sponsored football league at the age of 16. From there I graduated high school and immediately enlisted into the

U.S. Air Force. My father's leadership authored my drive, determination, and sense of loyalty and commitment. Those traits directly led to my succeeding in my career, community, and academic endeavors. My father's work ethic, love, and compassion was in the image of his faith in Christ Jesus. His love and passion provided for me, it protected me, it progressed me, and it caused me to be promoted. My goal in life now is to pass that image onto others.

18
Lottie Rayna Hicks, Senior Trainer

"A mentor should be open to listen without making a verdict, candid without being loutish, nurturing while providing guidance, and passionate to make a difference."
—Lottie Hicks

Whether it was being in the role of a manager, a trainer, or a mentor to my friends and family members, mentoring, encouraging, and inspiring others has always been a passion for me! My first experience serving in the role of mentor was about 15 years ago in a management position. As a manager, I learned that my role was not only to be a source of direction and support, but at the foundation of being a manager was being a mentor to others.

Coming from a large family of teachers in which my mother was a teacher, several of my aunts were teachers, and a few uncles were professors, I saw many examples of what it meant to be a mentor growing up. As I look back on my childhood and reflect on many lessons learned, I've realized that my mother was not only mom, but she was also my mentor.

According to Webster, a mentor is a wise and faithful counselor who can also be described as a coach, trainer, guide, educator, and the list goes on. When I think back to my role as a manager and my role as a trainer, this definition merely scratches the surface of what it means to be a mentor. To be a mentor, I've ascertained that one must truly have a sincere desire and passion for helping and watching others learn, grow, and achieve their best. That is what my mother has done and continues to do for me still to this day, which is my inspiration to do the same for others.

For me what has made my mentorship relationship with my mother so successful is being able to be completely open, honest, and vulnerable without fear of judgment, neglect, or ridicule. Well, you may think, "She's your mother, of course she would not judge or ridicule." Not necessarily. Like anything else, in order to be successful, you must have cultivated a high level of dexterity to ascend to a level that surpasses the norm.

My mother has always listened with an open mind, a caring heart, and an unbiased tongue. Whether I sought advice, needed a sounding board, or just wanted to solicit her opinion, she never once told me *exactly* what I should do. Instead, she created a path of reason by giving me things to consider while allowing me the freedom to openly express my thoughts, feelings, and opinions. At times when I'm sure my mother may not have agreed with my decisions, she never made me feel bad for not doing things *exactly* the way she would have done them. Instead, she chose to enlighten me through her own experiences and lessons learned. Her shared experiences never came off as though she were lecturing. I think a lot of that was due in part to the fact that she never led off the conversation with an anecdote of some kind. If the situation was an obvious wanton threat to me or others, her approach was vastly different. Usually in those cases, anecdotal commentary was somewhere around the corner. Still, on those occasions, I never felt judged or devalued. Instead, the answer or probable solution materialized right before my eyes followed by an empowering feeling afterward like the decision, the choice, was truly mine.

In order for a mentorship relationship to be successful, whether it's with a family member, friend, or colleague through work, individuals always need to be willing to make themselves available. Mentoring is truly an ongoing relationship that requires time and selfless giving of oneself by both parties. Mentees need to feel their mentor is someone whom they can trust and confide in and who is caring, honest yet fair, and supportive. The mentor needs to be willing to act as a catalyst of hope, positive change, and positive reinforcement. Additionally, a mentor should be willing to be open to listening without making a verdict, candid without being loutish, nurturing while providing guidance, and passionate about making a difference.

Through my experiences, the mentors I've seen throughout my life are individuals who live, speak, and operate according to their own credo. They are usually sought out by others for their remarkable wisdom, sense of compassion, and keen ability to make others feel valued and important. They possess a passion for teaching and generate a lending hand to help others see their potential and achieve their best.

Typically when I sought my mother out when in need of some mentoring, she always made sure that she was in a place where temptations to multitask were minimal and interruptions were few. During the times when I really needed her undivided attention, she made every concession to make that happen. When I needed her to be a mentor to me as the mentee, as opposed to mother to daughter, we did not cloud those conversations with topics that might derail us from achieving the objectives of those discussions. During these conversations, she allowed me to do the majority of the talking while she listened carefully and asked questions intermittently.

As a retired teacher, even to this day, my mother still has former students who have gone off to be political activists, doctors, lawyers, professors, entrepreneurs, and still seek her out for her mentorship. My observations have been that what she has done for me in a mentor role has been no different from what she does for her former students. In the beginning of a conversation, she spends most of her time listening and asking questions to make sure she understands the mentee's goals, challenges, obstacles, or whatever the situation might be. The art of listening is truly an art that she has perfected. I've met few people who have the ability to listen so intently that they can almost repeat back what you've said word for word. Another thing she does is avoid making assumptions or jumping to conclusions.

It took me longer to realize some of my mother's methods, which served to be added benefits for me in the future. For example, my mother challenged me to be more of a forward thinker and problem solver by cleverly walking me through a sequence of dialogues that resulted in possible solutions or ideas that I'm sure were obvious to her because of her own life experiences. Yet all the while after our conversations, I felt empowered, motivated, and encouraged! So I'm sure you're wondering how exactly she did that, right? Well there was a combination of things she did:

1. Assisted me in establishing a game plan and breaking down steps to get there.

2. Facilitated the process of my own explorations of possibilities, while coaching me through the pros and cons.

3. Recommended that I journal throughout the process and frequently revisit those thoughts and factor in how they may be a part of my ultimate game plan and potential lessons learned.

4. Recognized successes and mistakes and discussed lessons learned from both.

5. Provided constructive feedback and praise consistently!

Success was measured through the successful completion of stretch assignments and achieving stretch goals. Some of these assignments were created to challenge complacency and conventional thinking, overcome fear, or conquer assumed constraints. With each stretch assignment, I also learned a great deal about myself, which not only contributed to building my self-esteem but helped me feel more motivated to challenge myself even further. Furthermore, I found myself looking for opportunities to assist others who may have found themselves facing similar challenges so that I could be a mentor to them.

The stretch assignments enabled me to discover a skill level I never knew I possessed while learning and perfecting new skills that would make me even more successful in achieving my own personal goals. My mentor (my mother) always made it a point to celebrate those moments when I accomplished or achieved something that forced me to step outside of myself to try something new that on my own I might never have done. With each assignment came new goals and with each goal being accomplished came a level of excitement and inspiration that inspired me to want to do the same for others.

As a trainer, I have a multitude of opportunities to be a mentor to others, opportunities to network, and access to a variety of resources to help others achieve their goals and develop both personally and professionally. One of the goals that I make for those I'm mentoring is to create and establish new networks. Whenever possible, I make it a point to assist them in making those connections. In addition to sharing with a mentee my perspective based on my own experiences, I also recommend publications for them to read based upon their objectives. Like my mentor, I also assign stretch assignments and stretch goals, but I also like for my mentee and me to measure their successes together. We do this by periodically revisiting their journey of where they started and where are they now. Along that journey, we also identify what were the competencies needed and how they felt in those moments. As I mentioned earlier, when I was a mentee, it was important for me to overcome certain fears. My mentor helped me to do just that. The only way you can do that though is by tapping into those emotions. Sometimes we may not even recognize these emotions or are unable to identify for ourselves. For me, in the role of mentee, I didn't realize that I had certain fears until my mentor helped me to come to that realization.

One of the goals I assign to my mentees is to establish a contingency plan for dealing with those events or situations that may cause anxiety, fear, or other futile emotions. When those events or situations present themselves, I have the mentee journal them so we can manage and measure their progressions together. As a mentor, there is a certain level of personal satisfaction you feel from aiding in the growth and development of another person while being a witness to the achievements of the mentee. As a mentee, I was so grateful and appreciative to have someone care so much about me who took their own time, resources, and connections to be my guiding force.

Ultimately, it is because of my mentor that I was inspired to take a role many years ago to become a manager. There, every day, right in front of me were opportunities to be that source of direction and inspiration for others. Watching others I managed take on managerial positions were extremely proud moments for me! As my mentor always encouraged me to stretch and not allow myself to become complacent, I decided to step into a different role to reach a wider audience to make even more of an impact. The life altering experience for me has been that I finally feel like I'm in a role where I not only get the opportunity day after day to make a difference, but as a trainer and mentor to others I wake up every morning so grateful that I actually get paid to do this!

19

Rashida C. Walker, Educator and Student, Master of Divinity

"Another level, a journey to understanding..."
—Rashida C. Walker

Growing up, my biggest influence was my mother, who played and continues to play a large role in the person that I have become today. In essence, she was my first mentor, and she groomed me into a virtuous woman. As we know, it is hard to obtain everything that you need in life from one person; therefore, I was able to come across other mentors, such as spiritual mentors who are able to give me the spiritual guidance needed for the journey God has for me. In addition, I have come to learn there is no such thing as a permanent mentor or mentee. There are situations that life's journey will take you through that will require the leadership of others in many forms, settings, and environments. Whoever that person is who is designed to help you along the way, there needs to be a commitment from both parties to be honest to one another.

There are various types of mentoring experiences. Some mentors enter into the relationship for a short time while others may stay through a specific journey or time in your life. The role of a mentoring relationship can be represented in several forms: (1) teaching and learning, (2) leadership, (3) resources, and (4) family and community. In every aspect of our lives, there should be a form of teaching and learning. Teaching and learning are not created for a specific age, as anyone can be a teacher and a student. From a leadership perspective, the relationship should help the mentor inspire the mentees to be a positive influence in whatever environment they may find themselves in. As individuals grow and learn from others, they become a resource in order to build communities and inspire and transform families. Mentors are all around us.

Mentoring is about who you are, what you do, and how you live to make people listen. It requires you to live the life you have been called to live. Using the analogy of a fisherman, a good fisherman must use a rod, bait, and a net. In order to catch some fish, the fisherman must use bait on the end of the rod before casting it into the water. After the fish is attached to the hook from eating the bait, the fisherman uses a net to capture the fish. Mentoring is similar to this process. The role of the mentor is similar to that of the fisherman. What good are the tools for fishing if they are not used? Are you willing to put down your net to help pull up God's children?

As a mentor, you perform several roles: confidante, friend, supporter, and sometimes even a guardian. As with anything, you are equipped for every battle and journey in life. Just as with fishing, there is bait all around. Sometimes you will have to utilize your resources to find it. Through faith is where strength is birthed. Through struggle comes endurance. Because of trust and faith in God, we are able to survive. Survival brings laughter that comes from the spirit. Whether things are going good or bad, it is okay to laugh. To laugh means to Laugh About Unfortunate and Godly Happenings.

In order to become a successful mentor, you have to have an imagination of hope. The enemy of hope is the lack of imagination. We can no longer imagine backward, which is thinking of the way things used to be. Imagination has to include collaboration and the formulation of partnerships. Hope requires the ability to surrender and imagine. It is through imagination that the pursuit of dreams and living takes place. Nothing happens unless you imagine.

It is the role of the mentor to help with the direction that the road of life is leading a mentee. There is more to a reflection of a man than just walking in his footsteps. It is not the mentee's role to walk in someone's shadow but to be who he or she is striving and created to be. Mentoring without walls, although there are many boundaries, is not limited to the typical walls of a program. Mentoring without walls is a process that allows the masks to be removed from both the mentor and the mentee. These masks include, but are not limited to, unveiling the absolute truth of who you are as a mentor and even some of your experiences in order to help someone else grow and face life's challenges. It is a process that requires a mentor to be transparent and open to a mentee and involves being able to reveal the influences as a person, culture, religion, and even some of your personal experiences that have been tucked away in the closet.

Mentoring without walls requires the ability to break down barriers that separate us from each other. In other words, it aids in knowing the values of life by mimicking the actions of other people. There has to be love, trust, and respect. The greatest of these is love. Everybody needs someone to love. Mentoring is and requires a loving relationship. It is within love that we find out about ourselves, which enables us to help someone else. When you mentor another person, you will find the strength and all that you need even in your weakest moments and times of uncertainty. Often times God is all the help that we need. He can help us on our journey. Just as God has commanded us, we should love our neighbors as ourselves. Our neighbors in this case are our mentees. In order to love as ourselves, we need to understand ourselves. We must live our lives in accordance to the will of God.

The process of spiritual purification requires you to be vulnerable to the access of hatred. Hatred is not necessarily a negative attitude. Hatred could influence change and inspire a passion for commitment. Commitment brings about a sense of freedom. Freedom, as seen in various historical movements, is a change agent. This change agent is like taking a bus ride. While on the bus, we may get off at a stop prior to our final destination and get on another bus for a detour. However, we are required to get back on the same bus to complete our journey. The hardest part of the acts of freedom is getting "back on the bus." Once the action has taken place, you may need to get back on the bus to get to the place of transformation. The place of transformation is where you revisit the open wound in order for it to heal. This process will allow one to face a place of hurt to get to a place of love. Expressing this process through mentoring relationships engages both parties. In order for the journey to be completed, both participants need to ride the bus until the end of the line.

Self-awareness allows one to focus on a specific mission. Whether it is the mission of the mentoring relationship or the goal of self-purification, there must be a specific focus and direction. This process requires you to choose wisely because you may be called in other directions. It is easy for me to tell you to change. It is also easy for someone else to tell you how to change. However, the hardest part of change is for everyone to change themselves. Measuring the mentoring relationship captures the amount of change that has taken place. Change occurs when the process or person is different than its prior state of being. It is important to establish goals and objectives for the relationship that will capture change.

The mentoring relationship helps with the ability to connect souls with roles. Everyone has a place in a relationship. Often our roles are influenced by our roots in society. One must be able to understand the calling and action in order to help focus on direction. Mentoring is not about a name but a legacy that is left behind, a legacy that can carry on positive influences in order to help someone else. This legacy should be full of principles that can be adapted by others as they continue on life's journey.

Is the process of mentoring like the tree or the forest? Or could it be just a seed? Mentors often plant the seed but will never see the seed develop into a tree or even a forest. Like joy, mentoring is a contagious gift. The gift, when acknowledged and received, is an excellent model that can be shared throughout time. The model allows one to be affected in ways that can assist another person either consciously or subconsciously. When you are encouraged by a stranger who turns out to be one of your biggest supporters, it is empowering, rewarding, and uplifting. That person will often be the only one you may be able to call on in a time of need. Being able to witness as a life or even multiple lives are transformed by the work that is done by a mentor is gratifying. However, it is often done not for the recognition but out of love. This love and passion are driven by the experiences called life.

Being a mentor as well as a mentee is beneficial. Having experienced both sides, no side is greater than the other. Both are a gift. This gift that is never ending, life changing, and phenomenal is a way of leaving a legacy. It is a legacy that does not end when the season or feeling is over, but a legacy that has an influential impact on a person for the rest of his or her life. You never know the cost until you have seen the price.

20
Jerrell Riggins, Engineer

"Well Done is better than well said."
—Benjamin Franklin

My first experience as a mentee came through my
co-op educational experience in my junior year in college.
During this internship, I worked under the direction of the
chief engineer, who was a good person and very
knowledgeable and possessed leadership and management
skills. The critical points that I took away from this
experience were to write effectively to convey a message in
a clear, concise, and systematic way. It was clear that
during a training period, individuals must present
themselves well in every interaction with management,
peers, and administrative staff. An individual's appearance
must be professional and intact; be on time for work and
make sure you complete the assignments that you are given
and ask questions when you are not certain of what you are
being asked to perform. In working under the direction of
the chief engineer, it was important to have a good working
relationship, build trust, and let him know I was reliable
and could get the job done. The best part of this mentor–
mentee relationship was when he shared with me about

management operations in how to deal with employees and superiors. The advice was to be aware of the employees' strengths and weaknesses and seek out opportunities to help them get stronger in areas in which they need improvement. The other advice I received was how to respond to union versus nonunion situations. I remember Mr. MacDonald advised me not to speak negatively about unions if you are in management because your subordinates may be union and they are the frontline people you will need to get the work done. Always attempt to have a cordial relationship, understand the history of unions, and know that there are some positive initiatives that the unions were based on.

I had the pleasure of seeing his negotiating skills in meetings, seeing him get the outcomes he wanted, and seeing him use crafty techniques to smoke a person out if he thought the information was not quite truthful. This mentee relationship went well my first year, and I was invited to come back for my final co-op in my senior year as an undergraduate.

The second year, I saw that Mr. MacDonald believed in me, trusted that I would be on time for work, and knew I would do my best to represent the department and continue to grow and develop as a young engineering intern under his guidance and leadership. This led to some classroom training while at my internship and interfacing with consultants and other departments at the organization.

Having the opportunity to work in a professional environment and be exposed to the realities of what is expected of you and how to conduct yourself to give respect and receive respect in return was beneficial. You must produce and be on your "A" game to support your work, be knowledgeable about the subject matter, and answer questions sufficiently. Also, I received exposure to office politics and learned how not to get entangled and involved in the theatrics and never to bad mouth your supervisor with coworkers or others outside the department. This mentor–mentee relationship continued after graduation, and after I started my first job. Mr. MacDonald informed me of opportunities and openings 4 years later that were available for electrical engineers. Also, he has been good to speak to about pursuing a graduate degree and looking at a master's in business administration to complement the engineering degree in order to progress into management and get the background of how managers make decisions as to the direction an organization will go and financial decisions to expand or eliminate a program.

The other mentee relationship occurred with my pastor, who is a Harvard graduate with a PhD. The relationship revolves around spirituality, education, and thinking outside the box. My pastor stressed the importance of education, spirituality, and challenging yourself to come out of your comfort zone. He was committed to starting and supporting Black-owned businesses. This really helped me understand that if I want to improve my situation, I must have a strong belief in God, study His Word, and be a person of action. You must produce to get the desired results and satisfaction of seeing the fruits of your labor. The points he stressed to me were that religion is more than just a feel-good experience and you will have to be educated, knowledgeable, and learn how to transact business to make a life for yourself more abundant on Earth and not only in the aftermath of life. I credit him with my decision to pursue my PhD. He lives in Virginia and we are still in contact with each other. He was one of my critics in reading my statement of purpose in applying to Walden University. As a mentee, it is beneficial to have a good solid relationship with someone you respect, trust, and appreciate as a human being. This has been a positive experience and a worthwhile relationship that I value, and my current pastor knows him as well. Having the experience with someone who promotes high standards and challenges you to do more and not take shortcuts is like a wise man who builds his house on the rock. The foundation I have built for myself and following the blueprint instructions has helped me withstand the storms of life and have stability in the midst of the storm.

The final mentee relationship I will mention is the peer-to-peer relationship that is occurring in my pursuit to achieve my PhD in applied management and decision sciences at Walden University. The peer mentee relationship is very positive and I appreciate my peer mentor for the guidance, for sharing how to survive and do my best, and for knowing that I can and will succeed on this journey. The key is to not overwhelm myself and to take little chunks at a time with writing, stay focused, and set up a time management schedule to balance family, work, and school. Frequent interactions and check-ins have helped me to know I am not alone in the process and that my peer mentor has completed her PhD and this is a reachable goal. I must stay calm, not be anxious, and take one day at a time until I finish.

21
Eric Hamilton, Early Childhood Specialist

"Our deepest fear is not that we are inadequate. Our deepest fear is that we are powerful beyond measure. And as we let our own light shine, we unconsciously give other people permission to do the same. As we are liberated from our own fear, our presence automatically liberates others."
—Marianne Williamson

In my adolescent years, it was extremely difficult growing up without a father figure. During these years, I felt insecure and unsure about what it meant to be a man. I found it very complicated to understand myself as a male and the roles that were associated with my gender. I felt alone and did not know how to relate socially with others. I did not have anyone I could talk to about the feelings I was experiencing. My mom would have listened but I did not feel comfortable sharing my thoughts with her.

My mother was very influential in my upbringing. Through her teachings, she helped instill the values of hard work and dedication within me. My mother always told me, "Never wait or depend on anyone to do anything for you. Use the resources you have to get through the obstacles and challenges of life." A part of me believed the advice she gave, but another part of me knew it was not enough to subdue the inadequate feelings I had about growing up as a man. My mother did the best she could to offer me guidance and support surrounding the complexities of being a man. However, her help was not enough to fill the void of not having someone in my life I could relate to. I felt like a fish out of water. I needed a male role model who could teach me the attributes of manhood.

In August 1991, I attended a church service, and at this service I met Nathan Alverson. Nathan and I had an opportunity to speak briefly after the service. We talked about the need for everyone to feel like they belong and fit somehow into the puzzle of life. I was amazed at the conversation because it tapped into some of my inner thoughts of being alone and confused as an adolescent male needing direction. I was astonished at how Nathan uncovered thoughts I had been carrying for a long time and did not share with anyone.

The revelation of the internal thoughts prompted my spirit to connect with Nathan's spirit instantly. I believe he could sense the pain and confusion bottled up inside me. I believe Nathan also saw great potential lurking beneath the surface of my being and wanted to help me see it for myself. In him, I saw hope and wanted him to take me under his wing to teach me everything he knew about manhood. Internally, I knew Nathan would be an integral part of my life. He later agreed to become my mentor. Nathan became the father figure and role model I needed to connect me to a clear perception of what it meant to be a man. The mentorship between Nathan and I lasted 14 years and impacted me in a positive manner.

The relationship lasted for such a long time because Nathan embodied the ability to listen actively. He was always willing to hear about what I was going through without being judgmental. I felt comfortable opening up and talking to Nathan because he was very trustworthy over the years. I did not ever have to worry about him sharing confidential information with others. I could always depend on Nathan to be honest about the right direction to take in my life. He was a man full of wisdom and always willing to share his experiences to help me find my way. Nathan was full of patience. He realized helping a person develop takes time. Nathan was very passionate about growth and development. He always had my best interest at heart and wanted me to be successful. It is so profound to have someone in your life who is interested in helping you reach the maximum of your potential. Nathan helped me develop socially, emotionally, and academically.

The development I received from my mentorship experience did not have calculated formal guidelines. However, throughout our mentorship, every week Nathan and I would set aside a day to meet and fellowship. During these fellowshipping times, Nathan would expose me to various activities that typical boys liked to do. I remember the first time he took me to a football game. I was so excited. I did not know anything about football but I liked being in what I felt was a masculine environment. In my mind, all the men and boys there looked and acted more masculine than I did. That day I had a conversation with Nathan about manhood. I wanted to know what constituted being a man and what I needed to do to truly become one? His response changed my perspective about manhood and took away all of the insecurities I had. Nathan told me I did not have to become a man because I was already a man. The words he spoke captivated my soul and for the first time I realized how important it was to encounter and embrace the man who already existed within me.

I began to feel better about myself. Nathan continued to spend time with me. The fellowshipping times were not always just fun and games. Nathan taught me how to develop goals and timelines to ensure I was meeting my goals in a timely manner. Whatever goals were developed he checked to make sure they were completed within the designated time frame. Nathan shared with me the importance of having educational goals. He instilled in me the value of education. Nathan encouraged me to set my mind on going to college. Getting me to graduate with a college degree was a major goal in our mentorship. I knew I wanted to go to college but did not have a clue about what I wanted to major in. He helped me discover the gift of teaching that resided inside me.

Early on in our mentorship, Nathan noticed I had an innate ability to teach. He picked up on this quality through active listening and knew just what to do to nourish it. Nathan began to cultivate this gift by giving me opportunities to teach Sunday school and bible study at church. I became confident in my ability to teach. This confidence led me to choose a career in education.

After going off to college, Nathan made periodic visits to make sure I was making the best use of my time. He encouraged and guided me throughout the entire process. As a mentor he knew the importance of sticking by the mentee's side until the plan of action had been completed. Nathan was very pleased to see me graduate from college. He knew he had inspired me to do something that would open up doors and give me a chance to impart in others some of the skills and qualities he imparted in me.

Nathan also did not want to stop with me and our successful mentorship inspired Nathan to form a club for boys who do not have male role models they can count on. He mentors the boys just as he mentored me and the ultimate goal for all of the boys is for them to become college educated. Nathan's reward for being a mentor is intrinsic and tangible gains are not sufficient for the satisfaction he receives by witnessing the success of the boys he mentors. My mentorship with Nathan ended when I moved to another state. I had been under his wing for 14 years and we both realized it was time for me to take all that I learned through our mentorship and use the tools to become an agent of change and make a positive difference in the world by helping others.

I get this opportunity every day when I walk into my classroom to educate children. I am afforded and blessed with the chance to reach out and mentor children and instill in them the love of learning that my mentor instilled in me. As I did, children need someone to cultivate their gifts. They need someone who is concerned about where they are going in life and is willing to take the time to invest in their well-being. Children need some type of outlet where they are able to vent and get out their frustrations so that the challenges they are facing do not consume them. Had it not been for my mentor helping me find the confidence and strength I needed to stand tall and proud as a man, I would not be able to stand in front of children and encourage them to love who they are and help them to realize everything they need to be successful is already within them.

My mentorship experience truly changed my life. I transitioned from a shy adolescent boy who had feelings of inadequacy and insecurity to a man who is confident and believes anything is possible. I am no longer bound by my fears and I am free to continue to strive for bigger and better things in life. I learned through my mentoring process the importance of challenging myself to go beyond the physical limitations of my eyes and operate from the purity within. I am powerful beyond measure. I am grateful this life afforded me the opportunity to experience the powerful impact of mentorship. At some point in this life, we all need someone to take us by the hand and guide us through the rough places.

22

André Lynch, Healthcare Technology and IT Vendor Management

"We make a living by what we get, we make a life by what we give."
—Winston Churchill

According to Peter Northouse (2007), "Leadership is a process whereby an individual influences a group of individuals to achieve a common goal" (p. 3). Northouse further asserts that leadership is characterized by a power relationship that exists between leaders and followers (p. 2). It's this power relationship that bears the true essence of leadership. The success of both the leader and the follower are tied together and thus affect organizations. Success is thereby achieved in direct proportion to the leadership's sphere of influence.

Not only is mentoring a critical leadership skill, but leadership's greatest recompense and return on investment is demonstrated by mentoring others so that they can become leaders as well. Leadership can be equated to pioneering. Effective leadership focuses on the establishment of equity across social environments. One of the greatest pillars of organizations today is sound leadership. Amid times of ethical compromise and moral decay, society is challenged to answer the call of leadership. Mentorship is relative to leadership in that it provides the catalyst for individuals to become well rounded socially, physically, emotionally, spiritually, financially, and academically.

The concept of mentoring in organizations is a relationship that manifests characteristics that are often intense, occasionally intimate, and professional and are devoted to providing social support and development for the protégé's career (Carden, 1990). Most often the mentor is a senior in some regard to the protégé and whose advanced knowledge allows for the provision of upward mobility and assistance (Kram, 1978). Mentorship is demonstrated through a convergence of inspiration and information. The inspiration should challenge the natural tendencies and engage learned behavior. Essentially, this is what leadership does. It convinces individuals to do what they should do. Mentorship engages momentum for the process of personal growth and development. It is the response to the call to levels of engagement.

As a leader in both the military and a church setting, opportunities for mentoring have been plentiful. Both have allowed the impartation of knowledge and experience in such a manner that provided counsel, guidance, clarity, direction, and purpose. For me, mentoring begins with a genuine concern for the well-being of others and a desire to assist them through the course of life. It means being unconditional and allowing the opportunity to not only impart into the lives of others but to receive from them as well. In the last 20 years, I have had the privilege of mentoring and being mentored. Looking at the latter first, being mentored by sound, qualified individuals of substance has, in turn, set the course for me to do the same for others. From a ministerial perspective, I've had the privilege to be mentored by individuals whom I consider pillars of the faith.

Militarily, as both a unit training manager and first sergeant, I've been afforded many opportunities to mentor. After careful assessment of the individual protégé, I would discern his or her respective strengths and weaknesses and align those strengths toward successful completion of attainable goals. By accentuating positive characteristics, I encouraged protégés to give less attention to their limitations and to channel their efforts toward their strengths in such a manner that would benefit them both academically and professionally.

Similarly, as an ordained minister of almost 20 years, I mentor new ministers, both old and young, primarily through sharing my own experiences and shortcomings as a minister and by identifying pitfalls to avoid. This sharing allows them to relate better in the sense that identification through experience is now established. This identification now forms a better forum for continued communication because the mentees now view the mentor as a real person who, in many ways, is no different from themselves and the experiences they encounter.

In my own experiences with mentorship, whether as a mentor or a protégé, the hallmark of successful relationships has been a solid foundation of communicative and facilitative skills. Both of these critical components of the situational leadership style bear a strong resemblance to mentoring environments. Mentoring relationships evolve out of a method of communication between a mentor and a protégé. Though each has distinct roles, success of the relationship is based on participation from both parties who collectively work toward achieving a common goal. The mentor has the primary facilitative role but must simultaneously have a keen awareness of the needs and abilities of the protégé and adjust strategies accordingly. A specific tactic that may have been ideal for a previous protégé may prove to be of no effect to a current protégé. Timing is another key component in both mentoring and situational leadership instances. Precise movement is critical. Depending upon the maturity level of the protégé, moves must be executed appropriately at the direction of the mentor.

Leadership by example is the greatest motivational source, where the process begins and ends with a demonstrated synchronization between word and deed. Often, there is an imbalance of the two that compromises the integrity of solid mentoring relationships. People who walk the walk receive greater admiration than those who talk the talk. Situational leadership gives a new regard to mentoring relationships. Traditionally, mentoring has been regarded as "a relationship between an older, more experienced adult and an unrelated, younger protégé—a relationship in which the adult provides ongoing guidance, instruction, and encouragement aimed at developing the competence and character of the protégé" (Ragins & Kram, 2007, p. 5). Examples of the paradigm shift are clearly visible in today's organizations. For example, positions that have for centuries been traditionally occupied by men now welcome and operate under the expertise of women. There is a familiar phrase that states, "If you always do what you always did, then you will always get what you always got." In much the same manner, mentoring relationships have experienced a similar evolution. The mentor, in times past, was always an older individual. However, in today's society, with the recent advances in education, culture, business acumen, and technology, it is younger people who often mentor older individuals.

Mentoring has also been regarded as the "offering of advice, information or guidance by a person with useful experience, skills, or expertise for another individual's personal and professional development" (Harvard Business Essentials, 2004, p. 76). This definition parallels the ideals of the situational leadership model in that guidance is offered through the coaching and supporting quadrants of the model.

Lastly, mentoring involves a facilitation of learning toward long-term goals. Leaders who take the time to really know their employees in an organization are much like the mentor who puts forth great effort and concern for the protégé. By doing so, leaders act as mentors and organizational goals are accomplished with greater success.

As a training manager in the military, my job was to develop and manage training programs that measured individual performance at various levels throughout military members' career. I was tasked with ensuring that the skill sets aligned with duty position. Success was measured through successful completion of career development courses or formal professional military education courses. Although trainees were given a training program to follow, many instances involved charting paths that were not always traditional. The biblical account in the sixth chapter of the Old Testament book of 2 Kings provides an illustration through means of a battle against a Syrian army. An extensive military force of Syrian troops greatly outnumbered the Israelites and with all intent of complete annihilation, they positioned themselves to defeat the Israelites. Nevertheless, the leader of the Israelite army, the prophet Elisha, through exclusive leadership that focused on inventive strategies while adhering to spiritual principles and guidance, emerged triumphant. Elisha didn't resort to conventional means of warfare, but instead called for divine intervention that rendered the attackers powerless. As a leader, he resorted to a different means to gain ultimate victory. The greater the degree of leadership flexibility demonstrated by the leader, the greater the outcome for the organization. Because mentors are leaders, they must often employ these nontraditional tactics. I have often found that venturing away from the customary ways of mentoring has often yielded great success.

Impact and outcome are measured through goal setting. In a mentoring relationship, I establish goals based on what the mentee wants to accomplish. Sometimes I can see a greater potential for the individual than they see in themselves and encourage them toward possibly achieving a higher goal. Even in attempting to reach higher goals, I ensure that at least the goal they set for themselves is achieved. Sharing and learning are often the most intangible benefits I've encountered. Other successes include the successful completion of a course or program. In goal setting for mentees, I often learn something that I can either apply to my own life or use in other mentoring settings. I regard every mentoring experience as life altering in some way. Some instances are distinct whereas others are more subtle.

In conclusion, the role and responsibility of a mentor is a mighty one that is not to be taken lightly. The mentor lets the protégé know that failure is not an option and that significance in self leads to significance in society. My role as mentor is to instill the concept that integrity is never for sale. Through the demonstration of character and reputation, as a mentor, my intent is to become a beacon of light to what might appear as an impossible goal for the protégé and to share some sense of illumination in the life of protégés by pointing them to the highest vision possible for themselves and giving them an awareness of the unlimited possibilities to reach and fulfill their greatest potential.

References

Carden, A. (1990). Mentoring and adult career development: The evolution of a theory. *Counseling Psychologist, 18,* 275-299.

Harvard Business Essentials. (2004). *Coaching and mentoring: How to develop top talent and achieve stronger performance.* Boston, MA: Harvard Business School Press.

Kram, K. E. (1985). *Mentoring at work.* Glenview, IL: Scott, Foresman.

Northouse, P. G. (2007). *Leadership: Theory and practice.* New Delhi, India: Sage.

Ragins, B., & Kram, K. (2007). *The handbook of mentoring at work: Theory, research, and practice.* Thousand Oaks, CA: Sage.

23

Charles Edebiri, Business Architect
IT Source, Enterprise Services Cluster
Ontario, Provincial Services

*"A mentor is someone who knowingly and willingly accepts to
guide, counsel and assist the protégé to develop, improve and
make an impact on society."*
—Charles Edebiri

Mentoring is as old as creation. When Moses's
father-in-law saw all that he was doing for the people, he
said, "What's going on here? Why are you doing all this,
and all by yourself, letting everybody line up before you
from morning to night? . . . This is no way to go about it.
You'll burn out, and the people right along with you. This
is way too much for you—you can't do this alone" (Exodus
18:14–17). As I reflect on the characteristics of mentoring,
I realize that I have had mentors as long as I can remember.
Yet only in the latter half of the 20th century did the term
mentoring take prominence as one of if not the most
powerful dictum of contemporary leadership. As a young
man growing up in Africa, I can attest that mentoring came
in different forms and shapes. Beginning with my parents
who although obliged to nurture and provide guidance,
some of my greatest life lessons are not the things they told

me to do or not do but the time they expended on me and my family. In other cases, mentoring came from uncles, aunts, teachers, neighbors, and strangers who shared unsolicited life experience and cheered me on regardless of how insignificant an achievement I made.

During my university years, I had great aspirations but lacked specific goals, as is often the case with adolescence and young adulthood. Although I graduated with a first-class honors double major in mathematics and computer science, it did not seem to mean much. I had been blessed with many teachers who in collaboration with my mom and dad helped encouraged me to achieve one of the nation's top academic honors in my graduating class, yet none of these teachers made such a profound impact on me as the mentor I describe in the following few paragraphs.

After graduation and as part of my obligation and military service to my birth country of Nigeria, I was deployed as a graduate teaching assistant to Ogun State University. There I met a gentleman; Professor Otolorin, who was the head of the department of mathematics and computer science. His research interest was control theory and numerical solutions to complex differential equations.

I took great interest in his work and would often engage him in conversations on tensor theory and elasticity, which were the foundational theories for my graduate thesis. We soon became very good friends and would often go on long drives together. One day he invited me to visit with one of his old schoolmates. His classmate's name is Olaiya Orlando Ojo (Uncle Orlando), and he was at that time the director of data processing and computing at Nigeria's foremost oil and marketing company. He went on to be the general manager and chief executive officer for the corporation and recently retired as chief executive officer of Shell Liquefied Natural Gas Ltd. He is a Rhodes Scholar, a mathematician, and an alumnus of Imperial College, London. During our brief visit, he had asked some routine questions about my family background. As we left his office at Marina, Lagos, he invited me to visit him again in 3 weeks. I was momentarily curious but I never gave his invitation any further thought, as I was very young and adventurous. So 3 weeks later I boarded a commercial bus and took the hour and half ride from my post to his office. When I arrived, he treated me to a four-course executive lunch at his posh towers. He invited his executive assistant and some of his other protégés to meet with me. He certainly made me feel more important than I had ever felt. Then he began to ask me more details about myself and my aspirations. This man was and still is a man of very few words, yet he has an extraordinary ability to ask thought provoking and revealing questions. After about 2 hours with him, I had literarily been through an exhausting but rewarding lesson in critical thinking. I knew more about myself than I did before. More remarkably, a lifelong mentor–mentee relationship was born and two decades later he is still my mentor and one of my life benefactors.

While Olaiya Ojo has some of the finest personal qualities I know, the ones that have impacted me and contributed to the success of our mentor–mentee relationship the most are as follows. The first quality was his belief in me, as we all know the key role that the cheerleading pack plays in the success of any sports team. Winning, losing, or stalemate, they provide loud unrelenting chants of encouragement, unwavering belief, and support for their team, even when the most faithful fans can be despondent about their team's performance and begin to holler harsh words of criticism at the players. He has a knack for precision and diagnosing situations. Within a half hour of my initial visit at his office, he had instinctively recognized the untapped potential in me. He had taken great interest in me and was willing to take a chance with me by investing his gifts and talents. For this reason, he invited me to make a second visit. He has and continues to offer great wisdom through his far-reaching and varied experience. "Good friend, take to heart what I'm telling you; collect my counsels and guard them with your life. Tune your ears to the world of Wisdom; set your heart on a life of Understanding" (Proverbs 2:2). He exhibits great patience, empathy, active listening, and presence whether we are physically in the same place or communicating through real-time or asynchronous tools. Consistency engenders trust. Very early in our relationship, I observed with great interest how consistent Olaiya was in his way of life. This was one of the defining qualities of our relationship. He is a God-fearing man, devoted to family, and quick to offer his gift and talents for common causes and greater good. Respected and consulted nationally and internationally, he has an extensive global network of resources that he often makes available to his protégés when required. Uncle Orlando most certainly has what I personally need.

Uncle Orlando had very quickly discerned my innate desire to reach the pinnacle of formal education and contribute to the body of knowledge in the physical sciences. I do not recall any moment in time when I specifically told him that I wanted to attend graduate school or obtain a PhD. Perhaps it was the natural follow-up to my earlier successes in academia. When I was looking back a few years later, it dawned on me that the processes we put in place were to facilitate that unexpressed outcome. He asked me to go over to his alma mater; the University of Ibadan, also known as University College London, and obtain forms for graduate admissions and we were to meet at his office monthly to discuss updates and any issues of concern to me. I looked forward to those monthly meetings with much excitement, as you can imagine having the opportunity to be treated to executive lunch at one of the towers in Nigeria's business and financial district. I soon gained admission to study a master's program in operations research. Upon giving him the news of my admission, he issued monthly postdated checks to cover my living expenses for the duration of the program and suggested that I save my monthly graduate teaching assistant stipend. During one of our monthly sessions, he asked his chauffer to drive me over to the British Council where I could research colleges and universities in Britain and the United States. I subsequently made numerous return visits to the British Council and in the process made several applications to universities in England, Australia, and Canada. To obtain admission and scholarship to these universities, taking the Graduate Record Exam (GRE) administered by Princeton Education Services was required. In one of my informal calls to his office, I informed Uncle Orlando of my findings and the admission requirements. He immediately arranged for me to take the GRE exams in Kaduna, a northern Nigerian city approximately 800 km from Lagos. This journey took about 2 days due to meager road conditions. A few months later I had obtained admission, graduate scholarships, and teaching assistantship positions to 10 institutions in Canada, Australia, and England. Thus, my journey from Africa to the West had begun. In my euphoria, I traveled to my alma mater to inform old friends and acquaintances of my impending travel abroad. During that visit an unfortunate event happened that resulted in the loss of every dime I had been saving. This was a shameful event and I could not imagine discussing it with my mentor. I had seen him as a morally upright man of great wisdom. Although I felt comfortable telling him anything up to this point, this was an exception. I had displayed very bad judgment by giving my life's savings to an old classmate who informed me that he was in a business deal that could return over 300% in a few short weeks but that he needed to make the remaining payments. What would my mentor say? He expects better from me? So I decided to keep it a secret. After all, in a few short months I would be aboard a British Airways flight to London. But accountability time was around the corner at our next monthly meeting. This time he had arranged for our meeting to take place on a weekend at his residence. At the meeting I presented the admission and offer letters and we began to discuss the pros and cons for each institution. After considerable discussion we had settled on the University of Saskatchewan (Usask), Canada. The only problem was that the offer from Usask was one of the only ones that required me to travel on my own expense that would be reimbursed upon commencement of my program. At that point, my mentor remarked that I could use my savings to pay for the airfare and that he would make an electronic transfer of $1,000 directly to the international office to provide me enough funds until I received the first installment of my awarded scholarship. Twenty-five years ago, $1,000 could sustain a young student from Africa such as myself for a year or more. At this point, I was cautiously optimistic because I had lost all my savings. After my visit, I went back to my service post but was understandably disappointed. Later in the week I received a message that my mentor wanted to see me. I traveled to his office on Friday. During that visit he informed me that he had noticed that I was less enthusiastic than I had previously been about my impending travel. He wanted to know if there were any issues that I would like to share. At that point I had to let the cat out of the bag. I told him about the loss of my savings and how sorry I was for my bad judgement. I informed him that I planned to defer my admission until the next academic year to allow me save enough money for the airfare. He nodded in agreement and suggested that I use better judgement in the future. He asked me to remind him of the start date of my program at Usask. I told him September 4th and that I had planned to arrive at the university residence about a week before the start date. He then reached for his intercom and made a few calls and shortly one of his protégés walked into the office and offered to take me out for lunch. As we made our way to the restaurant, he made a detour into a travel agency and asked for one of the staff who apparently was also expecting us. Within a half hour I had been issued a ticket to travel to Mirable International Airport in Montréal, Canada. A few weeks later, a journey that would alter my life for good began.

We did not formally articulate a set of goals or measures to determine when and how the mentorship goals had been achieved. Our relationship had naturally evolved with the tacit goal of anything that helped me achieve my potential. Obtaining a graduate education was one of the objectives. Beginning with my admission to the graduate program in operations research in Canada, this goal had been achieved. Since my graduate program, I have made Canada my permanent home, married, had children, and named my son after my mentor. Uncle Orlando is godfather to my children. The mentoring relationship has allowed me to have a bigger personal vision and provided me much needed encouragement. I have benefited from my mentor's advice that helped me avoid many mistakes. I believe the relationship has been very rewarding and satisfying for my mentor to see me evolve into the man I have become.

24
Charles D. Shaw, PhD, Learning and Organizational Development Professional

"Inasmuch as any mentoring relationship is about the chemistry that exists between the mentee and the mentor, there also needs to exist a willingness to push the relationship outside of its comfort zone."
—Dr. Charles D. Shaw

I have been involved in some form of mentoring for the past 14 years of my life. These experiences have been characterized by the workable balance struck between both a process and a chemistry that results in the building of trust. There are three relationships that have been the hallmark of the successes that I have obtained personally and professionally. They have generated a greater sense of awareness and greater fulfillment. These three relationships were instrumental at various stages in my journey because they represent the stages of the life course. The passion I have for engaging in mentoring is anchored in my belief that relationships are nurtured through the mutual exchange of ideas, experiences, and stories. I also believe that when mentors have a commanding grasp of their own strengths and limitations through emotional intelligence, the potential for rewarding relationships manifests.

One of the most pivotal relationships that has contributed to my growth as a human being was with a woman I met my freshman year in college at Texas Southern University. She was my debate coach. Dr. Christie was the embodiment of the type of person I aspired to emulate in some regard. Dr. Christie and I established trust at a pretty early stage. Once, while we were on a debate trip in Seattle, Washington, she asked me to recite an excerpt of the literature that I was scheduled to compete with. After obliging her, she indicated her displeasure with both the selection of the material as well as the delivery. I recall her referring to it as garbage, as only Dr. Christie could. Though harshly delivered, 14 years later we still laugh about that night in the tournament hotel room when she referred to my work as garbage. I never presented her with garbage again. Our relationship spanned the course of my undergraduate studies, with her giving an ear, shoulder, and heart to some of the most formidable tasks in the life of a young college student. It was that experience in Seattle where we both realized that honesty and candor were deposits we needed to put into each other's emotional bank account.

An additional mentoring partnership that aided me in my doctoral studies was the relationship I had with my dissertation advisor. It was through an organic process that this relationship between us occurred. The relationship unfolded in the context of student and professor, but more importantly it was between two respectful and deeply caring persons. We shared a passion for improving the lives of the marginalized and less visible though organizational development work. To date, our greatest success has been the completion of my doctoral dissertation. I use this example as one measure of success. The other measure is that we presently have developed a lasting relationship that I anticipate being lifelong and we have agreed to coauthor papers and articles in the future. Through any intense and rigorous graduate work there is a world of emotion and intellectual juggling that can take its toll. I realize now that the one element that made our relationship so rich was that she always made the quality of time we spent together a meaningful learning experience.

The final mentoring relationship formed in an organizational context. It was with a gentleman who I have worked with in a corporate environment. In this relationship, no topics were off limits. We agreed that although we had been using a rather organic process, we needed to clarify how we would measure success. It was essentially the safety of security we created through the use of dialogue, an unapologetic honesty. It was also the ability to speak from one's own truth and to hold the space that one creates as a result of dialogue. We also agreed to not exercise modesty and there would be no judgment. Anytime we would operate outside of those parameters, we would open the door of inquiry. This was often uncomfortable yet developmental. We would meet periodically and he would give very detailed feedback on his observation of my behavior in meetings, in both large and small groups, and in the company of executives. Anytime I had to speak publicly, he would provide honest feedback on the audience's reaction and areas in which he thought I could improve. It was not only what he said, but also the manner in which he conveyed meaning. We had pretty clear ground rules around a few of Stephen R. Covey's 13 behaviors of trust:

- Straight talk
- Listening
- Clarifying expectations
- Confronting reality

With these in mind, we never left any conversation feeling as if we weren't heard or were unclear about the direction either of us would take. Although he was one of my mentors, he would often say "we were mutually mentoring."

These are three of the many relationships I have had the privilege of building and fostering over the past 14 years. Each relationship was unique to a different stage of my life and each provides memories and moments of profound growth. The willingness to be uncomfortable has led to very rich experiences that have left indelible marks.

Recommended Reading

Allen, T. D., Poteet, M. L., & Burroughs, S. M. (1997). The mentor's perspective: A qualitative inquiry and future research agenda. *Journal of Vocational Behavior, 51,* 70–89.

Anderson, J. (1988). Cognitive styles and multicultural populations. *Journal of Teacher Education, 39,* 2-9.

Aristotle. (350 BCE). *Metaphysics by Aristotle* (Trans. W. D. Ross). Retrieved March 14, 2010, from http://classics.mit.edu/Aristotle/metaphysics.html

Baldwin, J. (1991). *The fire next time.* New York, NY: Random House.

Blanchard, K., Hersey, P., & Johnson, D. (2008). *Management of organizational behavior: Leading human resources* (9th ed.). Upper Saddle River, NJ: Pearson, Prentice Hall.

Boote, D. N., & Beile, P. (2005) Scholars before researchers: On the centrality of the dissertation literature review in research preparation. *Educational Researcher, 34*(6), 3-15.

Brown, W. G., & Rudenstine, N. L. (1992). *In pursuit of the PhD.* Princeton, NJ: Princeton University Press.

Carden, A. (1990). Mentoring adult career development: The evolution of a theory. *Counseling Psychologist, 18,* 275-299.

Cooper, J. B. (2007, June). *Emotionally intelligent supervision: An examination of the role of* emotional intelligence *on the development of the supervisory working alliance.* Program presented at the Third International Interdisciplinary Conference on Clinical Supervision, Buffalo, NY.

Desivilya, H., Lidogoster, H., & Somech, A. (2009). Team conflict management and team effectiveness: The effects of task interdependence and team identification. *Journal of Organizational Behavior, 30,* 359-378.

Harkavy, D. (2007). *Becoming a coaching leader: The proven strategy for building your own team of champions.* Nashville, TN: Thomas Nelson.

Harvard Business Essentials. (2004). *Coaching and mentoring: How to develop top talent and achieve stronger performance.* Boston, MA: Harvard Business School Press.

Hunt, J., Osborn, R., & Schermerhorn, J. (1994). *Managing organizational behavior* (5th ed.). New York, NY: Wiley.

Kram, K. E. (1985). *Mentoring at work.* Glenview, IL: Scott, Foresman.

Kram, K. E., & Isabella, L. A. (1985). Mentoring alternatives: The role of peer relationships in career development. *The Academy of Management Journal, 28,* 110-132.

Maxwell, J. C. (2005). *The 360° leader: Developing your influence from anywhere in the organization.* Nashville, TN: Thomas Nelson.

Merriam-Webster. (1993). *Webster's third new international dictionary of the English language unabridged.* Springfield, MA: Author.

Milkovich, G. (1997). *Human resource management.* Boston, MA: Irwin McGraw-Hill.

Northouse, P. G. (2007). *Leadership: Theory and practice.* New Delhi, India: Sage.

Ragins, B., & Kram, K. (2007). *The handbook of mentoring at work: Theory, research, and practice*. Thousand Oaks, CA: Sage.

Roberts, J. (2002). The policy was perfect. *Security Management, 46*(9) , 92-98.

Simon, M. (2010). *Dissertation and scholarly research: Recipes for success* (2nd ed.). Del Mar, CA: Worldpress.

Smallwood, S. (2004). Doctor dropout. *The Chronicle of Higher Education, 50,* A10.

About the Author

Walter Ray McCollum, PhD

Dr. Walter McCollum is the Senior Director, Organizational Development, Sodexo, where he provides clients with organizational performance and transformation options in change management and project management to improve effectiveness and efficiency. He has been employed by some of the top companies, including Lucent Technologies, Booz Allen & Hamilton, Lockheed Martin, Science Application International Corporation (SAIC), and Capgemini.

Prior to working in the private sector, Dr. McCollum, a Desert Storm veteran, served 13 years in the U.S. Air Force, where he held various Air Force specialties in the areas of information management and communications. His military awards and medals include Air Force Commendation Medal w/1 Oak Leaf Cluster, Joint

Meritorious Service Medal, Air Force Achievement Medal w/2 Oak Leaf Clusters, Southwest Asia Service Medal, Humanitarian Service Medal, National Defense Service Medal, Distinguished Graduate Noncommissioned Officer's Academy, Military Citizenship Award Noncommissioned Officer's Academy, and the Office of the Secretary of Defense Junior Enlisted Member of the Year.

As a scholar practitioner, Dr. McCollum has authored and published three books: *Process Improvement in Quality Management Systems: Case Studies Analyzing Carnegie Mellon's Capability Maturity Model*, *Applied Change Management: Approaches to Organizational Change and Transformation*, and *Strength of a Black Man: Destined for Self-Empowerment*.

Dr. McCollum is also an adjunct professor at several universities, including Walden University, Upper Iowa University, and Argosy University. He holds a PhD in applied management and decision sciences with a specialization in organizational change and leadership from Walden University, an MA from Webster University, and a BS in psychology from the State University of New York.

CPSIA information can be obtained at www.ICGtesting.com
Printed in the USA
LVOW072217160412

277684LV00007B/7/P